John & Ellie,

Thank you for your

Friendship!

Best,

Behind in the Count: My Journey from Juvenile Delinquent to Baseball Agent

Behind in the Count: My Journey from Juvenile Delinquent to Baseball Agent

Written by KURT M. VARRICCHIO

Behind in the Count

Table of Contents

Dedication

For my loving wife, Amy;
my two boys, Corbin and Johnny;
and my foster parents, Sandy Evancho
and the late Joe Evancho.

Acknowledgements

First, I want to thank my wife, Amy, who encouraged me to complete the project I started several years ago. Her commitment and unwavering support were paramount. Next, I want to thank my foster mother, Sandy Evancho (pictured with me on the front cover), for collaborating with me and helping me identify those most seminal moments in my early childhood. Additionally, special thanks to the individuals who read the early drafts and provided much-appreciated feedback and input: Jim Callis, Glenn Geffner, Bruce Tatarian, Brian Brantley, Brett Murphy, Lynne Churchfield, Sarah Olin, and Scott Edinger. Your input was extremely valuable. I also want to thank Michael Ashley of *Ink Wordsmiths* who served as my editor and "coach" during this entire process. Finally, thank you to all of my family, friends and colleagues who supported me during this process, and to the many angels I met along the way.

Author's Note

The following is my life story, based on true events. In writing this book, I have utilized my best recollections of the conversations, events, and actions that have shaped me over the years. Many of these events I can remember like it was yesterday, while others are more distant memories. Either way, I remained truthful in describing the circumstances and persons involved. Furthermore, while I used the real names of most people in this book, I have consciously changed certain individuals' names and defining physical features to protect identities. I have not had recent contact with many of the people who are mentioned, but I have vetted other individuals and resources to confirm information related to them. Since I do not know if some of them are still living, incarcerated, or fully rehabilitated, I do not want to bring any undue and unsolicited attention to these individuals, especially if they have moved on with their lives in a productive and positive manner.

Preface

I waited for the boom. High above the Fort Lauderdale Beach, 4th of July fireworks exploded across the coastline, entertaining thousands of cheering families. Surrounded by concrete walls and a one-inch thick glass window, I could only glimpse the streaking pennants in seclusion, unable to hear the signature thunder claps. Instead of celebrating Independence Day with friends and family, like most other red-blooded American 11-year-olds, I stared at the Florida night sky, the silence in my isolation cell deafening as cold beams of color twinkled in the distance.

On that summer evening in 1982, I pleaded for a new beginning: *just give me one more chance—a real chance—and I will say goodbye to this lifestyle forever.* I was tired of the handcuffs, the shrieking red and blue lights, the sprinting police chases. I was tired of my older brothers kicking my ass, tired of my mom's inability to control them. I was sick of fending for myself on the streets and being forced to run away. Not even a teenager yet and I knew I had already missed out on childhood. I didn't want to lose out on adulthood too.

No one could do the hard work for me. Not disapproving cops, overworked teachers, callous juvenile hall guards or other Juvie misfits overwhelmed by the system. For change to happen, it had to come from me. *I* needed to prove people wrong. To lift myself out of this juvenile hell,

I had to show the naysayers I deserved to be called by a name instead of a number.

The following pages chronicle the moments that shaped me, challenged me, and nearly killed me. With each small triumph over adversity, I learned how to 'win' at the game of life, and with each setback, I learned how to improve myself. I wish to tell my gritty, unvarnished truth so it may serve as a beacon for other children suffering through difficult times. It's you downtrodden, in particular, I wish to reach: those kids getting thrown in backs of squad cars, getting locked up when you should be outside playing. I also hope adults reading this will be better prepared to understand youth classified as "at-risk."

The following stories include the obstacles and decisions that shaped my personal and professional life. Despite what everyone says, it's my firm conviction we *can* shape our destiny. No matter the circumstances, we *can* impact the outcome. There will always be opportunities; it's up to us to recognize and seize them. Make no mistake: this book cannot cure your problems, nor guarantee your success at any level. Nothing can do that but you and your efforts. This book will, however, give you a practical understanding of what worked for me. By learning from my mistakes and achievements, you will be better able to face your own unique life challenges.

Chapter One: Hard Times

In the fall of 1980, I was a soda-bottle-collecting nine-year-old. I scoured streets, open fields, and garbage cans, collecting glass soda bottles to cash in at the local Winn Dixie Supermarket. Often, I would make up to $12 at a time.

One afternoon, I was walking next to a 7-Eleven at the corner of 66th and Stirling Road. Inside the store, fluorescent lights lit up mouth-watering treasures: Twinkies, Doritos, Kit-Kats, and all kinds of healthy snacks for a growing boy. Crumpled newspapers and wrappers from a tipped trash can littered the cracked sidewalk.

As I dug into the garbage, an older gentleman approached.

"You collect bottles?" he asked.

"Yeah." I proudly held up my bag as proof. "It's an easy way to make money."

"Well, you know, there's quite a few bottles in the field over there. Follow me, I'll show you."

I had seen this guy a few times outside the shop and around the area so I figured it would be safe to follow him. We walked away from the 7-Eleven, crossed Stirling Road, and started trekking down toward a field littered with dense trees. Venturing further into a clearing, I could no longer hear cars buzzing nearby. After a few more minutes,

I looked back as the entrance into the field grew more distant.

"Are we there yet?" I kept asking, scouring the dirt as I did the street, looking for more bottles.

"Almost there. Just follow me."

At last, we reached a dense patch of trees in the center of the woods. Garbage was strewn everywhere. Empty cigarette packs and beer cans covered the ground. It looked like this area had been used by homeless people, prostitutes, drug junkies or anyone else needing somewhere to crash. Misunderstanding the situation's gravity, I became annoyed. I hadn't seen any bottles I could actually use.

"Well, where are they?" I asked.

I will never forget the man's answer. He turned to look at me with evil in his eyes. "I'm going to kill you." He flashed a devilish grin. "But first I'm going to fuck you."

As soon as he approached, I screamed so loud I was sure people back at the convenience store could hear me. No one did. The trees swallowed my yells, the sounds dissolving into the mud.

He grabbed my shaking arms with his long, clawing fingers as he undressed himself. Terrified, I cried out more, begging for help. No one came. He held me down to undress me next. I struggled, flailing to get loose.

And then a strength I never knew kicked in. Adrenaline surged through me. I broke free from his grip and dove through trees, tripping over tree stumps. I could have outrun a cheetah at that moment. I escaped the clearing, suffering only minor scratches and bruises. 7-Eleven's peeling paint had never looked so comforting as my feet smacked pavement seconds later. I spotted someone getting out of a car in the parking lot. *They could save me if the man returned.*

I changed my mind. I wasn't sticking around. I curved around the building and onto the nearest side street. I had dropped my bottles but I didn't care. I raced home with rubbery legs, one eye peeled behind me, wondering if he was still after me.

Once inside my house, I latched the door shut, then sat on the kitchen floor with my back against a cabinet. I stayed there panting with the image of his evil grin stuck on repeat.

I didn't tell anyone about the incident. I was too embarrassed. Instead, I plotted my revenge. In my neighborhood, you always sought vengeance on those who wronged you, or *tried* to wrong you. I wanted to kill this guy, so I packed a butcher's knife and headed back to the clearing the next day. *This guy was mine.*

I carefully planned my attack. I would tell him I made a mistake. I shouldn't have run away. I was going to convince him that I *wanted* him to rape me. I was going to act so convincing he would undress himself, then lie on the ground. Then I would cut him up. I gritted my teeth, thinking about the other kids who weren't so lucky; ones who hadn't gotten away. I would avenge them.

The next day, I retraced my steps through the woods.

"Hey man!" I yelled from outside the bushes. "You in here?"

No response. I edged in further, scanning the clearing for movement.

"It's me," I continued. "The kid from yesterday. I made a mistake."

My right hand tightened on the knife hilt. Careful not to rearrange the T-shirt camouflaging it, I crept in closer, pulling back branches one at a time for a better view.

"Hey man, you here?"

I made my way through the brush until I returned to the scene of the crime. No one was there.

I never got my revenge, for which I'm thankful. Aside from the fact I'd have committed a heinous crime, I also may have failed. Failure would have probably meant being raped and killed. My decision to return was lose-lose, but vengeance, combined with immaturity, blurred my ability to see the potential consequences.

While I wouldn't wish such a horrific experience upon anyone, it taught me a valuable lesson. I will always remember my fear in facing a deranged molester, but I will also always remember how I reacted. I didn't fall to pieces. No one was there to save me, yet I escaped. In hindsight, I shouldn't have been naïve enough to trust a questionable stranger, but I was a kid and sometimes kids (and adults) make bad choices. It's how we deal with our mistakes—how we deal with adversity—that defines our character.

This encounter taught me resilience, hardening my determination to avoid future vulnerability. Such vigilance has stayed with me throughout my life. In restaurants, while most people study menus, I study exit signs. I always sit facing the door so I can see everyone coming in. Walking in a crowd, I think about what I would do if a psycho started shooting everyone with a machine gun. Snap decisions can save a life, and I want my decisions to be as well thought out as possible.

Horrifying things happen every day. Rather than collapse in helplessness or wallow in self-pity, we owe it to ourselves to rise to the occasion. I was nine years old when

I first overcame a deadly situation. This particular experience is but a microcosm of the danger and adversity I would continue to face as a troubled kid growing up on the streets of South Florida. Through extreme hardships, I learned to pull myself out of helplessness and vulnerability.

I am not alone. You too, can do this in your own life.

Chapter Two: Game Planning

Goals for a typical eight-year-old boy might include winning a neighborhood game of tag, not getting yelled at by his teacher, or figuring out how to get the newest toy. My only goal was to exist another day.

Every morning I woke up on guard against the threat of roaches crawling in my bed and up my wall. Soon after waking, I would venture to the kitchen on high alert. Tiptoeing to reach a mug and spoon, I was careful not to wake the dragons, my twin brothers: Tommy and Eddie. If I ran the tap too long or accidentally clinked a glass, I opened myself up for a brutal beating. Stepping lightly, I would carefully grab the can of *Ovaltine* from our sparse pantry, then mix it with lukewarm water. Stomach rumbling, I would seek out more food if I could before trying to leave the house unseen.

Steven, my next older brother, stayed out of trouble and left me alone but the evil twins made it their mission to abusively "discipline" me. Tommy, the meanest, never made it past the ninth grade, and his emotionally stunted, moronic brain had a hair trigger temper. If I was lucky, I would get out the door before he and Eddie awoke.

I usually spent my days running around the streets doing whatever I wanted. Often times, this included breaking into vehicles for arcade money, shoplifting candy from the local grocery or convenient stores, and stealing money from the wishing well at The Ark Restaurant on Sterling road in Davie, Florida. This was how I lived my life. I was eight and already knew how to survive day-to-day. I "made" my own money. I made my own meals, and sometimes I literally made my own bed wherever I would lay down for the night.

Despite my unenviable situation, I was gaining an education no text book could ever provide. I was learning how to "game plan." Basically, I woke every morning and thought to myself, 'How do I survive today? What can I expect? Should I go to school today? If so, I would get a free lunch. Do I need more money? If so, how could I get it?'

My survival depended on my ability to answer these questions. Whether I knew it or not, I created my own hierarchy of needs. My primary goal was always basic survival. My intermediate goals included eating enough, avoiding Tommy and Eddie, and most importantly, keeping myself safe for one more day.

I always formed my strategies alone. I didn't have close friends. My best friend used to be a guy named Mark but one day my older brothers and Mark's older brothers decided it would be fun to watch Mark and I fight. Mark and I were boys back then. The last thing we wanted to do was hurt each other but Tommy and the others insisted. The day it happened Mark and I stared at each other for about ten minutes, pleading with our brothers to leave us alone.

Fighting had always been a defensive act for me. I didn't want to be an aggressor, like Tommy and Eddie. My brothers couldn't have cared less. They wanted to be entertained that day. Much stronger than Mark and me, they twisted our arms and wrists and pushed us into each other as they encouraged us to throw punches. It was like poking at a dog to make it growl, and eventually, we fought. I was the more experienced fighter due to my home life, so I won. But winning wasn't a good feeling. It meant losing my best friend. Mark disappeared from my life after that. It's hard to be close to someone who punched you in the face and kicked you while you were down on the ground.

But let's back up a moment. How did I get there? Why was an eight-year-old forced to strategize for his own survival?

As I understand it, my family's collapse occurred soon after my father's death. A devoted and reliable blue-collar guy, my father, Thomas Cosmo Varricchio, Sr. worked as a plumber, first in New York, then in Florida. In addition to serving in the Plumber's Union in South Florida, he held leadership roles with the *Sons of Italy* and the local *Moose Lodge.* After his shift, he always came home to spend time with us kids. According to my mother, he never shied from giving us affection. In the few photographs I've seen of him, my brothers are sitting in his lap and there's a loving gleam in his eye.

My parents met at the Moose Lodge in Hollywood. My father frequented this hangout when he wasn't working and was smitten by a beautiful young woman named Joan Marie Higgins, my mother, who was 38 years younger. Unfortunately, I never had an opportunity to get to know my father as he died of cancer two months before my second birthday. At the time of his death, he was sixty-nine. Prior to marrying my mother, my father had been married and raised three other children, all of whom are at least 40 years older than me.

In spite of the massive age difference, my parents somehow made it work. Our Hollywood home was modest, but sufficient: a 3-bedroom, 2-bath single story residence on the corner of 66th Avenue and Perry Street. It was large enough to house my parents in the master bedroom, my older twin brothers in one bedroom, and my brother Steve and me in the third bedroom. Looking back at photos from when my father was still alive, I can tell the house was kept tidy and my parents showed pride in ownership. Once my father died, however, things turned drastically for the worse.

Growing up, my mom was known for her looks, even winning beauty pageants. After several children, however, her 4'11" frame took on a few extra pounds, making her look less like a glamour girl and more like a typical, short, overweight Irish mother. Perpetually frugal, she still made sure to provide gifts on birthdays and Christmas. One particularly bountiful year, my brothers and I made four or five trips to her car to gather garbage bags filled with holiday presents. Of course, we weren't permitted to look in the bags, though we all wanted to.

My parents had four children together—all boys. Tommy Jr. and Eddie are both five years older than me, and Steven is almost three years older than me. I was the fourth and final child. Within a couple years of my father's death, the once orderly corner-lot deteriorated into a pigsty. Roaches, spiders, and other insects infested it. I remember waking up some nights with cockroaches scurrying over my face, arms, and legs.

Slap!

I'd look over to see Steve's hand retracting in the dark. "Cockroach, Kurky," he'd say.

I'd mutter a quick "thanks" and fall back sleep. Bedtime as usual.

In addition to the cockroach problem, our roof threatened to collapse from incessant rain. With storms prevalent in South Florida, we made a routine of positioning bowls and trash cans beneath leaking roof holes, but nothing prepared us for the first week of September, 1979.

Hurricane David was the first major hurricane of the annual season. Forming off the coast of West Africa, it became a category 5 hurricane—the highest rating on the Saffir-Simpson Hurricane Scale. Though weakening prior to hitting South Florida, Hurricane David's winds gained enough strength to rip chunks off of our roof, leading to gaping holes. Flooding soon followed, leaving us scrambling to determine our next step. My plumber father wasn't there to fix the problem and my mother was—well, overwhelmed. We did our best to assembly-line the process of bucket-carrying and floor-protecting, but nature was merciless on our small home.

After the storm passed, my brothers and I went outside to assess the damage. Toppled trees and power line poles lay slain in the streets, making the roads look like the intra-coastal waterways of Fort Lauderdale. I rolled up my pants and walked toward the street. The water was about 12-18 inches deep, and though it only came up to my knees, I knew enough to be wary of Florida's indigenous wildlife—alligators and water moccasins—so I was on high alert. At eight-years-old, this was my first time experiencing the true power of nature's wrath. Peering at the vast destruction made my young mind reel.

Hurricane David's devastation foreshadowed worse things to come. Our home was severely damaged, and my mom had neither the money nor the know-how to fix it. It's easy to think of our degenerating home as a metaphor for our rapidly decaying home life. For the next few years, rainy season after rainy season, our house took on more water. Leaks became so prevalent that despite our bucket collection, salvaging the floor as well as significant parts of the structure, became futile. At a young age, my brothers and I were forced to live in a collapsing house, rotting from the inside. Walking through the kitchen in inches of water after heavy thunderstorms became another new normal.

While my mother worked an odd job here and there, our primary income came from my father's social security, totaling $196 a month. Trying to stretch this meager amount to cover the food, clothing, and shelter needs of four growing boys proved nearly impossible. My father's death essentially paralyzed my mother. Grief, not just from my father's death, but also from the loss of Joey, a deceased son from a previous marriage, tore at her. Joey died in a motorcycle accident when I was six years old, and the double tragedy threatened to unhinge my mom.

I never questioned my mother's love, but she wasn't operating at full capacity, or even close. Prior to marrying my dad, her first husband abused her terribly. Her brother abandoned her and she harbored resentment at missing out on what she considered to be a normal family existence. Just like our roof, giant, gaping holes tore at my mother, leaving her unable to function normally. She had a rough life, but always fought to survive. I now wonder if I could've done more for her, and I've often felt guilty over my decisions. Still, the reality is, I was a child back then with little parental guidance and lots of problems. As time went on, our fortunes only sank further. Daily storms, within and without, worsened as our home life crumbled.

Chapter Three: No Brother's Keeper

Because my father passed away so early, my brothers and I were left with no true father figure. I recall my mother dating men periodically, but these were hardly guys we could look up to for advice and guidance. Naturally, the twins felt they had to assert themselves. The problem was there could only be *one* man in charge. As Tommy and Eddie fought a war for the "Father of the Household" title, Steven and I became collateral damage. Financial stress and impulsive violence comprised the terrain. Fists, handcuffs, belts, and even hand-tools were often the artillery.

Hostilities came to a head one Saturday morning. I had started my day with a few hours of cartoons and *Land of the Lost.* In one of the few times I can remember from my childhood, I actually felt relaxed. For the time being I wasn't constructing pragmatic strategies for survival. I was just hanging out, being a kid.

Then Tommy called my name.

My stomach dropped. I wanted to run but knew I had to go to him fast or I was in for a serious beat-down. Heart pounding in my chest, I crept outside.

Clearly mad about something, Tommy sat on his knees, working on his bicycle. Placed upside-down on the seat and handle bars, the wheels were in the air. He kept spinning the wheel, making it go faster and faster with quick slaps from his palm. Tommy was always pissed off about something so I wasn't surprised by this latest mood swing. Still, the manic wheel spinning looked especially menacing so I decided to back away toward the house, hoping he wouldn't notice my feeble attempt to flee.

"Kurky, grab that wrench. And hold this fucking tire bolt."

"What wrench?"

"That one, you stupid little fucker." He pointed to an instrument on the floor by his knee.

I grabbed the tool, holding the bolt in place while he loosened the other side with a pair of pliers.

"Hold the fucking wrench, Kurky."

The pliers kept slipping, stripping the bolt. I tried my best to hold the bolt in place, but Tommy couldn't figure out how to loosen the other side. My knuckles turned white from gripping so hard. Tommy's wrench slipped. He hit his hand on one of the wheel spokes and exploded.

"Damn it, Kurky! I told you to hold the wrench."

"I am holding the wre—"

Before I could finish my sentence, Tommy threw his wrench at me, clocking the side of my head. I grew dizzy, seeing two Tommys, two bikes and two wrenches. I thought I was going to puke on his broken bike. Tommy showed no remorse, just continued screaming. If this kind of thing happened to another kid, they might've gotten treated at the hospital for a concussion. Not in my house. A hospital visit might alert the authorities.

To avoid any more of Tommy's abuse, I took off running as soon as my head cleared. I often ran away from home. The way I saw it, I really didn't have a choice: either be alone on the streets for the day or risk a beating from the twins. Since I was so much younger and smaller than them, there was no way in hell I could ever fight back.

Beds on the street were easy to find once you stopped being choosy. On one occasion, my "mattress" was the roof above a laundromat at a local shopping plaza. After scouring the alley for a way up, I formulated a plan. Reaching my small hands around a dumpster's edge, I rolled it to the building directly under a half-sized ladder descending from the rooftop. Once on the dumpster's top edge, I hoisted myself up, balancing on top of the thin dumpster walls. Reaching the ladder, I leaned forward, kicking the dumpster back as far as I could, about four to six feet, to cover my tracks. If I didn't take such precaution, chances were good the police or some other third party might notice something awry and deduce someone was on the roof.

After kicking the dumpster away and climbing to the top, I crawled on hands and knees across the pebbled rooftop to find the best spot to sleep. There were multiple large vents and air conditioning units I used as walls to avoid detection as well as to block the wind. Once situated, I could finally relax. Other kids might have felt scared looking up at the night sky all alone, but I felt safer here than at home. Out here beneath the stars, emptiness meant freedom. I could sleep without being woken by Tommy's fist or a biting bug. After a couple of hours, I fell asleep wrapped in newspapers.

The following day, I decided to return home. I walked up to the front door—and stopped. I felt like I was returning from a vacation resort.

As soon as I eased open the door, my mom squeezed me into a tight hug. "Kurky! You're home."

For a second, I felt welcomed. Then, I peeked my head around my mom's arms and saw Tommy approaching.

"Where the fuck you been? You nearly gave mom a heart attack, you stupid shit."

I braced myself, not realizing Tommy was about to introduce a whole new form of discipline.

"Get over here. *Now.*"

Tommy yanked my 75-lb body from my mom, pulling me through the house as he searched for something. He dragged me in and out of the bedrooms, the kitchen, and the bathrooms. I stayed mute, watching the skin on my wrists turn crimson under his grip. At last, he found what he was looking for: steel handcuffs.

While I wasn't happy to see the cuffs, I wasn't too scared either. I had been handcuffed by my brothers on more than one occasion. Once, Tommy and Eddie handcuffed me to the living room sofa while they left so I wouldn't "go anywhere and do something stupid." At the time, they created a crude type of shackling/tethering including cables, padlocks, chains, and handcuffs.

Attached to their invention, I could still walk to the bathroom, twenty feet away. If I really stretched the cables and my hands, I could open the refrigerator and barely grab whatever was within reach. They held me captive that day for over eight hours without food or water. Now, seeing the steel contraption in Tommy's hand, I expected a similar lock-up. I guessed wrong.

Tommy dragged me outside. In our backyard, we had a large avocado tree in the corner, about 40-50 feet tall. The tree had a large branch, approximately 12 inches in diameter, stretching about 6 feet off the ground. Tommy grabbed a chair from the porch and put it under the branch. Then, he placed one of the cuffs on my left hand

and demanded I climb on the chair to grasp the branch with both hands.

"But Tommy, the tree's covered with red ants. They're going to bite," I whimpered.

"This will teach you to run away."

Usually I masked my pain in front of my brothers to avoid more torment. Now, I wanted someone to hear my fearful cries. I called out to my mom to save me. In response, Tommy threw my right hand over a branch, placed the second cuff on it, then removed the chair, leaving me to hang. He walked away without another word.

Gravity became monstrous. My wrists were supporting all of my body weight as the handcuffs cut into skin and my hands began to turn purple. Pain pulsed through the space under my arms, into my upper back, onto the tops of my shoulders, and finally in the nape of my neck. But this didn't even compare to what was coming. I looked up in horror as the fire ants began their assault. In seconds, my arms became a stream of red. Hundreds of ants climbed over open skin, stinging me multiple times.

I screamed and screamed. After what seemed like an eternity, my mom finally came outside. It was one of the first, and only times, I saw her switch flip. On rare occasions, my mother could be assertive, even capable of beating my brothers. She snatched a chair from inside, placed it under my feet, then ordered my brother to undo the handcuffs so I could get down. He trudged his way over and reluctantly un-cuffed me. I sprinted to the hose and showered myself, blasting off the red ants with water.

Later that day, I ran away from home again. I spent the afternoon wandering around town, eventually making my way to the Ark Restaurant in Davie where I snatched some coins from the wishing well to pay for lunch. Behind the Ark was a series of canals where ducks congregated. It was quiet and peaceful there so I decided to kick back and relax as I ate a cheeseburger and fries. The tranquil moment was soon interrupted, however, when a manager caught sight of me and demanded to know what I was doing there. Once again, I took off running. This time for home.

As soon as I returned, Tommy started beating me again. Punching, pushing, kicking. I tried to fend him off, but he was much older and tougher. After struggling for some time, he used one hand to grab me by the back of my pants, then the other to stronghold my neck. Like tossing a bag of potatoes, he chucked me into my bedroom. I hit the door jamb first. My shoulder slammed into the side and I fell to the floor, screaming in pain. Tommy had finally done some real damage that wouldn't heal with ice. He broke my collarbone and I was in a cast for months.

Each time the violence escalated in my house, my perception of normal changed. Each beating took a toll. Living in fear hardened me. I had to make decisions to protect myself. Living on the streets and engaging in criminal conduct might seem like the wrong course of action to someone else. To me, it was the only alternative to the hell I endured at home.

Chapter Four: Robbing and Stealing

My mom's favorite child was born in 1978 to her and her boyfriend, Chuck. My little half-sister, Marie, was my mom's pride and joy. Perhaps it had to do with missing Joey, her first-born son that died, or feeling fed up living with a bunch of rowdy boys—whatever the reason—my mom threw everything into adoring Marie. As soon as she was born, all of my mom's attention went straight to her. I never felt jealous of my little sister. In fact, she became my personal security project. Just like me, she needed constant protection from my brothers and I was determined to give it to her, no matter how small I was. Despite my ambitions, however, I couldn't protect her from my mom's driving.

One day my mom took the three of us on an errand in her yellow Ford LTD. Mom, Marie and I sat in the front without seatbelts on, Marie in the middle. After stopping at a truck-stop gas station, we headed back out on uneven road. Marie was just two years old, and I bounced her hand as she stared out the windshield with wide eyes.

Suddenly, the car careened into a huge, water-filled pothole. All three of us flew into the dashboard. Blood ran down my forehead but I forgot all about my own pain when I heard Marie cry. She, too, had smacked her little head on the dashboard. Seeing she was confused and scared I smiled down at her, making funny faces so she wouldn't think about the scary thing that just happened.

Mom slapped me across the face "What the fuck are you laughing for?"

"I was trying to distract her, I—-"

"Stupid jerk. What kind of asshole laughs at his own little sister for getting hurt?"

"No, Mom. I wasn—" She hit me again and pulled Marie into the lap. By now Marie was bawling. My mom tried to soothe her with a lullaby. In between verses, she glared at me from the corner of her eye. I shut up. I knew my place in the family then.

Becoming more invisible to my mother, I started taking advantage of my independence. Without structure, I began doing what I wanted. Although I can't recall the exact date I first took something that didn't belong to me, I do recall what I took. Strolling through a shopping plaza's parking lot on Sterling Road near 66th Street, I peeked inside car windows. At first, I didn't intend to do anything mischievous, I was just being nosy.

I noticed a pattern: various amounts of change in center console cup holders. I stopped when I found a car with the front windows down. As I peered further inside I saw an ashtray full of change—and an opportunity I couldn't resist.

I walked around the car three times, keeping an eye out for its owner or other shoppers. After several minutes of circling my prey, I went in for the kill. Reaching my hand in the window, I grabbed the change, dumping it into the makeshift pouch of my t-shirt.

I felt a sense of accomplishment as I ran away. I now had enough coins to get through a day of pinball at the video arcade. With nobody harassing me, those next few hours were intoxicating. Not only that, I had enough money to enjoy life for once. I was on top of the world.

That win fueled more break-ins. With every electrifying click of the door handle, my confidence soared. I started breaking into three or four vehicles a day. I never had to even smash a window or pick a lock because so many people left their doors unlocked or windows opened. In addition to keeping money in ashtrays and center consoles, I learned people would also leave money in their glove compartment, under their seats, or beneath their sunshade.

I became efficient at getting in and out of vehicles, honing my craft over the next several months. While I was getting better at criminality, I was also getting a bit careless. One day, I was inside a vehicle, cramped on the floorboard, searching for coin glints, when the vehicle owner and his wife suddenly walked up behind me.

"Hey, kid! What are you doing?"

Instincts kicked in. I whipped around, kicking the man in his leg before darting off. But he was quicker than me. I barely made it to the gas station curb 60 yards away when he grabbed me by the shirt collar.

"What were you doing in my car?" he demanded to know.

His wife caught up to us within seconds.

I played innocent. "Just trading my pennies and nickels for some quarters so I can play video games. Here, you can have all of them if you just let me go."

The owner's beet red face looked hostile, but I noticed sympathy in his wife's expression. She looked me over. I was dirty. My shoes were worn down. My clothes were ripped and stained. I knew if I could gain her kindness, she would tell her husband to let me go.

I began whimpering, mustering up fake tears. "Here, take my change. I'm sorry, I just wanted to play video games and the store wouldn't give me quarters." I continued to whimper, looking away from my captor.

Bait set.

"Honey," said the wife. "Let's just leave the kid alone. There's really no harm here. I feel sorry for him."

Fish hooked. Now I just had to reel it in.

The husband loosened his grip on my shirt, but he still wasn't through with me. "I ought to turn you into the police to teach you a lesson."

Uh-oh. The fish was fighting. Time to crank things up a bit.

"No. I can't go back home to my big brothers. They beat me every day. I can't go back there."

The waterworks were really flowing now. Real Academy Award winning stuff. I could see the wife agonizing over my act.

"Just let him go, babe. He learned his lesson."

Hesitantly, he removed his hand. I ran off—with his change. *Fish landed.*

So far in my criminal pursuits, I had learned about stealing other's property. This experience, however, taught me about emotional manipulation. After my escape, I reconsidered my tactics. After all, robbing cars was risky. I feared getting caught again and not being as fortunate. Accordingly, I turned to a different type of criminal activity.

***

It was a sunny afternoon in Hollywood, Florida. At eight-years-old, I should have been in school, but I decided to skip because, quite frankly, I didn't care to go that particular day. This was how I did things growing up—my way. Although the bus would pick me up right across the street from my home, often times I would get off at school and simply leave campus as soon as I arrived. Other times, I would walk towards the bus stop only to hide behind a car while the bus left, then walk down the street and enjoy the neighborhood for the day.

I'm not sure what prompted me to go up to this particular house in my neighborhood, but I knew I was in need of cash to keep me busy for the day at the arcade and buy lunch. As I approached, I knocked on the door. Although I had never done this before, I knew I probably shouldn't have entered a house if someone was in it.

I had my script memorized. I would knock on the door. If nobody answered after the first set of knocking, I would knock again. Then, if they had a doorbell, I would ring the doorbell and knock. I would spend a minute or two ascertaining whether or not anyone was home, often times peering through a front window. If they were home, the script would go something like this:

Me: Hi. I'm sorry to bother you, but I was just wondering if you would like me to cut your grass. I cut grass to make money.

Owner: No, I think we are fine.

Me: Okay, sir (or ma'am). Thank you. Take care.

I also devised a backup script in case some homeowner asked why I wasn't in school on a weekday in the middle of the morning. I would either say I was homeschooled, went to a private school and got the day off, or this was part of a school project. Even at the age of eight, I knew it was important to roll answers off my tongue. It helped my credibility, which ultimately warded off suspicion. I couldn't let a homeowner report my truancy to the police, throwing a wrench into my plans.

As I said, on this first day, I approached the house and knocked. No answer. I knocked again and again. Nothing. I rang the doorbell twice. I peeked through the front window but didn't notice any movement. I knocked and rang the doorbell one more time. Nobody was home.

Now I could move to step two. I walked around to the back of the house, looking for neighbors. Though I was sneaking around, I still had to *look* like I was supposed to be there just in case someone did see me. *Acting like I belonged was key.* People needed to assume I had every right to be there. To accomplish this deception, I assumed the role of a family member visiting from out of town, arranging a look of believable confusion on my face.

Once my role was set, I checked the back door—locked. The sliding glass doors were also locked. *What now?* I checked the windows. *Voila!* They were cracked open. I removed the surprisingly easy screen and lifted the window.

My heart was in my throat as I crawled through. I could hardly breathe. I worried about all kinds of disasters. *What if the owner was in the shower and didn't hear me knocking? What if they were in the bathroom so they decided to ignore the unexpected visitor? What if they came home in a couple of minutes?*

Question after question popped into my head. I shook them off and got to work. I left the back door ajar, then checked each room. I wanted an immediate escape route just in case I ran into an unsuspecting person. After a quick scan, I focused on my objective: cash and cash only. I had no reason to steal televisions, stereos, radios, or any kinds of home goods or appliances. I was only looking for money and took any and all I found—including change.

The entire process took about three minutes. With money in my pocket, I closed the back door, then exited the same window I climbed in. The other key was to make the home appear as if nothing ever happened. I put the screen back on and double-checked it. Then I peeked around the front to make sure a new car wasn't in the driveway. Certain the coast was clear, I calmly walked to the front of the house, onto the sidewalk, and into the street.

I don't remember how much money I acquired from that first house but it was way more than from any car. It kept me busy at the arcade for most of the day, allowing me to buy some lunch. *Not a bad haul.* Unfortunately, it was the beginning of what would soon become a very bad habit.

Chapter Five: Juvie

At nine-years-old, I dabbled in elementary school. To me, school was merely an option, albeit one including a free breakfast and lunch since my family was on the free lunch plan. In the months following my first home burglary, I began to expand my criminal activities. I also continued to break into cars to steal money. I even began breaking into businesses to steal money. Whenever there was opportunity for financial gain, I seized it.

Things were getting out of hand, but I chose to ignore the dangers. On some occasions, I would even break into three or four homes in one day, most of the time on the same street. I had become more efficient with each conquest and my confidence grew. On this particular day, I decided to pass on the free school meals. Instead, I took a trip to a local strip mall off Taft Street, about a mile from Driftwood Elementary.

I walked around the strip mall parking lot, looking for unlocked cars. Finding a few good opportunities, I swiped the change, then headed for the arcade. However, on the way to the arcade, I found an even more interesting surprise: an unattended, unlocked bicycle outside a *Zayre* department store. Never one to pass up a good opportunity, I took the bike without thinking. I rode away from the store, then remembered my original plan to play video games. I pedaled back to the arcade, about 200 yards from *Zayre*. The enticing prospect of *Space Invaders Pinball* must've softened my critical thinking skills because I left the bicycle in front of the arcade just as I had found it: unattended and unlocked.

About 30 minutes later, a police officer entered the arcade. *Great. He's going to nab me for truancy. Now I'll have to return to school and it's only 9:30.*

Instead, the officer spoke up. "Who does that bicycle out front belong to?"

As the proud owner of my recently acquired asset, I retorted, "It's mine."

Bad move. Suddenly, the original *and rightful* owner stepped into the arcade. He stood behind the cop, looking me up and down.

"Son, step away from the video game," the officer said.

I decided to play dumb. Turning back to the pinball machine, I continued to flip away at the metallic ball while jostling the machine back and forth. "Why do I need to do that?"

"Step aside from the game. And come with me."

I couldn't do that. Mired in my game, I was dominating! The officer asked me once more to step aside and come with him. Realizing I had to be cleverer about my deceit, I turned away from the game, spinning lies. "I borrowed that bike from a friend."

Seeing as the owner was clearly not my friend, I quickly realized I needed to qualify my last statement.

"Okay, okay. Look. No one was near the bike. I just had a quick joy ride with it. I was going to return it."

The owner stood with his arms crossed, shaking his head in disbelief. The cop's eyes turned to ice.

"Actually, officer. I have a medical condition. I can't walk. I can only stand up to play pinball. When I need to walk, I need a bike. I need it for my safety."

Upon the word, 'safety,' I felt a familiar tug on my wrists as the officer cuffed me. Life was about to get interesting.

***

Although I had prior dust-ups with the law, this was the first time I was actually booked into custody. Throughout the trip to the police station, I remained smug and confident. *This is not a big deal. They're just trying to scare me. Those assholes—pulling me away from* Space Invaders *to make their point.*

At first, I thought they booked me just to teach me a lesson. After the scary fingerprinting and mugshot, I was certain they would take me back home. I was wrong. When we left the station, I noticed we were not going in the direction of my home.

Naturally, I spoke up. "Hey, man, you're going the wrong way. My house is back towards Sterling."

"Well, son, you're not going back home today. You're going to Juvie."

Those words hit me like a freight train. "Juvie" was slang for the Juvenile Detention Center. I will never forget how I felt at that very moment. My stomach tightened. I began to sob. I asked the officer if he was sure I had to go and begged for one more chance. I told him I would be good and never break the law again. My requests fell on deaf ears and I was booked into the Fort Lauderdale Juvenile Detention Center.

If I thought my brothers' fists were an uninviting entrance, that barbed wire gate was a close second. It immediately closed behind as we entered. Fearful thoughts rushed through my head. *Does my mom have any idea where I am? What about my brothers? What would they do to me when I get out? Will I get out?*

I couldn't shake the what-ifs. The fear was too powerful. I knew I was going to be the youngest kid in Juvie and other punks would see me as an easy target. *What if I get beaten up? What if someone tries to rape me or molest me? What if I get jumped by a bunch of kids?*

It didn't take long to understand life inside a correctional facility. As I recall, the Ft. Lauderdale Juvenile Detention Center was divided into four separate Mods. Mod B-1 ("Mod 1" for short) was comprised of younger boys, typically 13-15 years-old, which I was placed in. Mod B-2 was for older and bigger kids, typically 16-17 years-old. Mod B-3 was for "special" kids: those with severe emotional and/or physical disabilities, making them "severely at-risk" for being assaulted by other inmates. The final Mod was G-1 for female inmates, regardless of age.

Entering Mod 1, I realized the not-so-prestigious honor I now carried in my family. I was the first one of four boys to land in a correctional facility—and I was the baby. Although it was my first time inside, I knew I had to look confident. As I walked in line with the other newbies, I puffed out my chest, kept my head upright, and occasionally made eye contact with the inmates. Though scared as hell on the inside, I couldn't let anyone see it. Fear showed weakness, and weakness in this setting meant trouble.

The intake process was not only intimidating but downright humiliating. We stripped down to nothing as guards watched, then stood there as we lifted our privates.

"Lift your head up and open your mouth wide. Stick out your tongue. Lift up your tongue," the guards demanded.

The intake officers looked in our mouths, up our noses and under our arm pits. Then, the most unforgettable moment of the process occurred.

"Bend over, spread your cheeks and cough," instructed one of the guards.

What the hell?

After a brief pause, I acquiesced and did as instructed.

Once the physical inspection was complete, we had to take a quick shower—in front of the other newbies. Then they provided us special shampoo designed to kill lice while monitoring us to make sure our scrubbing was up to par. After the shower, we changed into standard-issue clothing, received bedding, and marched down to our Mod.

Chapter Six: Ambush

At nine-years-old, I was assigned to Mod B-1 (normally for youths, aged 13-15 years old). Entering the cell block, I immediately took a lay of the land. The front entrance was beside the guard viewing station, an enclosed office containing the controls running and monitoring the Mod. The guards would typically sit behind thick windows, separating themselves from the inmates for observation. They were specifically looking for potentially developing situations.

Next, I turned my attention to the living area's layout. The Mod had a large, central area, surrounded by individual cells. The first half contained several chairs and hard couches. The furniture faced the television, which sat in front of the guard area, anchored high on the wall near the ceiling. Bathrooms and showers were located immediately to the right of the guard area. The second half of the general population area was wide open, excluding a few tables where inmates played cards and dominos.

As for sleeping arrangements, each cell contained two beds and, thus, housed two inmates—with one exception. The first cell nearest the bathroom was the largest in the Mod, housing seven inmates. This was to be my new room where I would gain my first lesson in surviving the system.

While being escorted by guards to my specific cell, I noticed several inmates staring at me. I didn't know what to make of this at first, but my instincts kicked in. I knew something wasn't right. I placed my sheets on the bed second furthest to the back because another kid took the last bed in the row of seven. As I walked toward the cell door and the main Mod, I noticed five individuals huddling close to the cell entrance. I felt their eyes fixed on me. Though their staring made me uneasy, I acted like I didn't notice and approached a chair in front of the TV.

Watching *Bugs Bunny* with other inmates for the next hour allowed me to relax a bit. I tried to take my mind off the gang of five by focusing on the others' comments about the cartoon characters.

"Damn," one kid said. "Road Runner fucked that coyote up!"

"Hell nah," yelled another inmate. "That dumbass coyote deserved to get his shit lit up."

The comments continued throughout the cartoons that morning and into the afternoon with guys cracking jokes, jumping up, yelling, laughing out loud and just being exceedingly entertained by the childish cartoons.

Chuckling at my neighbors' play-by-play couldn't stop me from worrying for long about those five individuals huddled in the corner. Once they caught me looking at them, I quickly turned away, returning my attention to the screen. Something unnerved me about those guys. I didn't know what would come of it—not until later that evening.

At last, a guard called, "Lights out."

As each inmate headed to his cell, I observed which kids were going where. Some of the ones I had talked to in the last few hours seemed pretty cool so I wanted to know where they were sleeping. I continued watching their steps as we left the main Mod area with growing dismay. The guys I felt safe with, those that made me laugh, were leaving in the opposite direction.

Shuffling to my cell, I noticed the group of five still congregating—and still keeping an eye on me. Then they came right for me.

Shit.

I pretended I forgot something and walked back to the television area. I planned to let the group of five head to their cells, then I'd go to mine. My objective was to avoid confrontation, especially since I was outnumbered by older and bigger kids.

Noticing a guard by the bathrooms, I decided I needed to use the facilities. *Maybe they'll be in their cells by the time I come out. They won't mess with me if I'm by a guard. I hope...*

My plan worked! No one was around when I exited the bathroom. The five had disappeared. This time, I speed-walked back to my cell, proud of outmaneuvering them. But as I entered my cell, my heart stopped.

Holy shit.

The group of five were my cell mates.

I tried to play it cool by not making eye contact as I hoisted myself into bed. I knew they were watching my every step, but I pretended not to notice as I slipped under the covers. The scratchy fabric made my arms itch, but I wanted every inch of me covered so I tucked them tightly around the entire mattress, pulling them up to my neck. Holding the covers close, I made sure my backside was flat on the bed.

A few hours passed and I fell asleep. Suddenly, I heard banter between my cellmates. I kept my eyes closed as I listened to them.

"Wake the motherfucker," one said.

"I'm tryin', nigga, but he ain't moving."

"Shake his ass then."

Someone grabbed my shoulder, then another slapped my leg. I tried to ignore them.

"We know you awake, motherfucker, so get up."

"Yeah, get your ass up, bitch."

"What do you guys want?" I pretended to be annoyed instead of scared out of my mind. "I'm trying to sleep."

Marcus, an intimidatingly muscular black kid, came into view. Though technically he fit into this Mod's age range, he was bigger than the sixteen and seventeen-year-olds in Mod 2 and probably could've run their show too.

"Listen up, little man," Marcus said. "We been trying to wake you for a while."

"Yeah, okay." I tried to keep the tremble out my voice. "Why? What do you want?"

"Well." Marcus smirked at the others. "We were trying to fuck you in the ass, but you have shit all in it so we gotta figure out somethin' else."

Terrified and not knowing what to do, I suggested they talk to my cellmate and turned over to go back to sleep. This last request really pissed off the group. I could practically feel the floor move as they grew louder, shifting their weight in agitation.

"Let's fuck this cracker up!"

A chorus of "hell yeah's" and "go, nigga" filled the cell. They squeezed in closer as Marcus grabbed me by the shoulder, rolling me back to face him.

"No no, little man. We don't want him—we already had him. We want the new kid. That's you."

Fear stole my breath away. I was locked in a steel trap. No one was coming to protect me. I had to talk my way out of this situation. "Well, I have poop in my butt so that's not going to work. I'll allow you guys to do it tomorrow and make sure I'm clean. Just let me sleep tonight."

I was trying to buy one more night because I knew I wouldn't be in this cell the next day once I told the authorities. I thought my reasoning was valid to let me off the hook, but Marcus was having none of it. Meanwhile, the other kids continued to scream for my blood.

At last, Marcus called for quiet so he could tell me my two options. "I guess I can let these guys have their way with you now or you can do something for me that'll get 'em off your back. What you wanna do?"

Before I could guess what he was suggesting, the others erupted again.

"Let us fuck him up, Mo."

"Yeah, I'm counting to five and if this motherfucker don't give you what you want, I'm gonna bust his ass."

Another one pounded his fist into his hand. "One...two...three...."

"Okay, okay," I said. "What do you want me to do?"

He told me. I knew I had no alternative to remain safe. What transpired next was not only humiliating, but the hate I carried inside from that moment on truly tested my resolve, almost derailing my future.

Chapter Seven: Aftermath

I always tell shy or introverted people, "If you can't physically help, be the kid in the back of the cell." The one in mine saved me from future harm and though I never got to thank him, I will always be grateful he spoke up. Feigning sleep during the incident, the next morning he told a guard what happened.

Minutes later, the guards brought me into a room with a man in a suit.

His questions came fast and furious.

Suit: Did you know the assailants?

Me: No.

Suit: Did you try to resist?

Me: Yeah, of course.

Suit: What did they do or say when you tried to resist?

Me: They said they were going to kick the shit out of me—that they would beat me up and hurt me really bad – maybe even kill me.

Suit: Were you afraid?

Me: Yeah. There were five of them and they were bigger and stronger than me.

Suit: Can you tell me what they made you do?

Me: *(Silence as I stared at the ground in shame and humiliation.)*

Suit: Kurt... Can you tell me what happened? Specifically?

Me: *(I continued to stare down at the ground in silence.)*

Suit: Kurt... It's okay to disclose things to me. We want to hear your story so we can make sure these young men are dealt with appropriately.

Me: *(Still quietly staring down to the floor, I finally spoke.)* They said they would hurt me real bad if I told anybody anything.

Suit: Of course they did, but you are safe now. You won't be back in that situation again. I promise you.

I looked up at him. I took in his striped tie. His briefcase. The supply of pencils and pens at the ready by his side. The guards stacked beside him.

Where were you assholes last night?

"Kurt," the Suit repeated. "You're safe now. I promise you."

Promise me? I don't know you and you're making promises to me? My own family has made promises to me forever and they never kept them. Why in the hell should I trust you?

I sat there, staring at the floor as the Suit prodded me along, hoping I would provide more information.

At last, I raised my head. "How do I know for sure you're going to protect me? How do I know these kids won't find me later and kick my ass?"

"You will be kept in an isolation cell." He picked up a pen as if to finalize his point. "And nobody will get to you again."

At last, I disclosed the details to him. I said them slowly and deliberately, like I was explaining a medical procedure instead of sharing the worst moment of my life. Verbalizing each word, my emotions swirled from sadness to trepidation, then finally fury, rage, and desire for retaliation. Experiencing sexual assault is tragic to anyone, but especially a young child. It often leads to the train going off the tracks at some point in the victim's life.

Once the Suit recorded everything, they took me to my protected isolation cell. The following day, I was released. Soon after, a trial commenced in which I testified against Marcus. The whole time on the witness stand, I was so fearful Marcus would one day find me and complete the job he started. Though scared of what Marcus might do to me, I knew what I wanted to do to him: *kill him for humiliating me.* For years, vengeance ate at me. I often thought about tracking him down myself and exacting my revenge on him.

The result from the trial? They extended Marcus's sentence in Juvie, then sent him to prison after he turned 18. I received a $35 witness check for testifying.

But back to Juvie. After meeting with the Suit, I left, determined never to return. From first-hand experience I now knew what others before me professed: Juvie is a shithole filled with derelicts and deviants bent on inflicting pain and humiliation to unsuspecting and weaker inmates. They had done enough to me. I was going to get my act together and start abiding by the law. Instead of jacking cars and houses, I would go to school every day, do my homework, and steer clear of trouble. It was time for me to turn my life around and I was on my way. At least, for a few months.

Chapter Eight: My Disastrous Introduction to Baseball

Growing up, we couldn't afford to go to baseball games. Instead, we used our TV as a portal to the stadium. On game days I staked out the house, making sure my brothers were gone. Then I would adjust the rabbit air antenna to keep the signal, fashioning rods out of aluminum foil or sneaking into my mother's closet to bend an old, metal coat hanger for the job.

If I was lucky enough to both avoid my brothers and get our TV to broadcast the signal, I would happily settle in for the treat, squeezing between stained portions of our couch or sitting on ripped carpet. Catching a Yankees game on WPIX via our small, black-and-white television was the only thing that could occupy me for three straight hours. My mother knew this fact, so she encouraged me to watch games as it also offered her an anxiety-free window.

The first weekend after my Juvie stay, I glued myself to that TV set. I wasn't even paying much attention to the social worker assigned to my case, flinching as she rounded each corner of our disheveled home. At one point, though, I noticed her talking with my mother in the kitchen, so I decided to eavesdrop on them during commercial breaks.

"Kurt needs something to do," I heard the social worker say. "Otherwise he's going to return to running around the streets all day."

My mother took the hint and signed me up for the local baseball league. Though she was the kind of parent who merely dropped me off, never staying for games or practices, I still wanted to prove myself to anyone who watched, and most importantly, to myself. I showed up to my first practice in shorts, a t-shirt and MacGregor sneakers, all purchased from Kmart the previous year. My outfit, paired with a fielding glove from the Salvation Army, immediately marked me as the poor new kid. That didn't faze me. I was ready to play, paying little attention to the other kids' brand-new cleats and fresh leather gloves.

I had a chip on my shoulder. After watching baseball on television for so long, I thought the actual playing part would be easy. I didn't take into account the learning curve or the importance of practicing. I quickly grew frustrated but pressed on. Though the coaches probably knew I would struggle since I never played before, I was unaware of this fact, thinking I would be successful in our first game.

My first at-bat went like this. The first pitch came. Swing and a miss. "Strike one," said the umpire.

Okay, he got lucky on that one. The second pitch: swing and a miss. "Strike two."

Damn it. Hit the ball! I tightened my grip on the bat, my eyes fixed on the pitcher. *Okay, you little punk. Just throw that pitch again.* The third pitch: swing and a miss.

"Strike three. You're out."

In seconds, I became part of the real game—the one in which you don't even hit the ball. I was not happy. I scowled at the cocky pitcher. Returning to the dugout, I angrily kicked up dirt clods.

"Nice swings, Kurt," yelled my coach encouragingly from his third base position. "And don't worry about it. You'll get him next time."

Yes. I will get him next time—this kid got lucky.

My second at-bat was a bit more memorable, but not for good reasons. As I stepped up to the plate, the catcher started trash-talking. "Let's go, Bobby, strike this kid out. He's not going to hit it. Just throw it down the middle."

What the hell is this? He's talking smack about me? I'll show him.

Once again, I tightened my grip. I raised my hands, ready to give this next pitch a ride. The first pitch came: swing and a miss.

"Strike one."

"See? What'd I tell you?" said the catcher to his pitcher. "This kid can't hit. Just throw it in there and let him miss it again."

I looked at the catcher in disbelief. *He was allowed to say this stuff?* Recalling my oath to improve, I bit my tongue—a new tactic for me. When the pitcher threw the second one I purposely didn't swing. I wanted to show the catcher his incessant chatter didn't affect me.

"Strike two."

Strike two?

I stared back at the umpire. "That was a strike? But I didn't even swing."

"If it's right down the middle and you don't swing, it's a strike, son."

Damn. I knew that, but I was too focused on the catcher's smart mouth. Unfortunately, my flub only made the catcher cockier.

"He doesn't even want to swing now, Bobby," the catcher laughed. "He's scared of you."

Bobby smirked at that. Now I was pissed off. I was going to hit this next pitch off Bobby's face. I tapped the bat on the plate to show them I meant business, then raised it to my shoulder. I was going to crush it.

"C'mon Bobby. Throw it right here. He'll miss it. I guarantee it."

The pitch came: swing and a miss.

"Strike three. You're out."

The catcher cheered. "Woo hoo! Told you, Bobby, this kid has nothing."

I turned around, feeling the bat's heaviness in my hands. "Look here, buddy. If you don't shut your mouth, I'll shut it for you."

"Oooh, now I'm scared."

"You should be, punk."

The umpire heard the exchange and sent me to the dugout. My third base coach followed me. "Kurt, you have to let that stuff go." He squatted so we were on eye-level. "He's just trying to get you out of your game."

"He's trying to tell me I suck. I don't like that."

"Don't let it get to you. You'll get another at-bat to prove yourself."

I sat on the bench, waiting. By the 5th inning I had been listening to the catcher's snide remarks to more and more of our players. To make matters worse, we were losing and I did not take losing lightly. My threshold for the catcher's badmouthing was nearing its limit. Once it was my turn again, I returned to the plate with my bat, staring him down.

"Don't start that chatter stuff again," I said. "You've been warned."

But just as soon as these words were spoken, the catcher started in again. "C'mon, Bobby. You got this kid. He already struck out twice. Just throw it in here."

My fingers choked the bat like I was squeezing the life from a chicken. The first pitch came: swing and a miss.

"Strike one."

"Yeah baby." The catcher screamed. "He's doing it again. Kid can't hit."

It's okay. The coach told you to ignore him so ignore him.

"Throw it in here." The catcher punched his glove. "Easy out. Easy out."

Pitch two: swing and a miss.

"Strike two."

"Ha-ha, we got him now. This kid has nothing. He's nothing."

This last statement—the one about me being "nothing" I remember most. It's the comment that sealed this kid's fate that day.

"You better shut your mouth you piece of garbage, or I'll shut it for you.," I said.

"Whatever. Just get in and hit. Or, should I say, *try* to hit."

"I mean it. Don't push me."

The catcher just scoffed and the umpire told us to settle down. I stepped into the batter's box, more focused on the catcher's mouth than the next pitch. When it came, I swung and missed, striking out for the third time.

As soon as I struck out, the catcher opened his mouth. "Ha! I told you he wouldn't hit it."

I dropped my bat, hitting the catcher with a right hook across his head. Though he had a helmet on, I knew he felt it. Then I jumped on him, punching him anywhere he didn't have padding or gear. I ripped his mask off his face.

"I told you, motherfucker, to shut your mouth." I kept pummeling him. "I told you!"

I was still raining blows on him when the umpire and coaches pulled me off. I had tried to turn the corner. I had tried to take the high road but couldn't muster the maturity to carry out the task at that young of an age. As to be expected, the umpire tossed me from the game. Parents and players looked on with shock, probably more entertained in those thirty seconds than by the entire season. After publicly scolding me, the coach told me to run laps until the game ended.

"Why should I have to run? That kid started it."

"No excuses. Go do it."

To make matters worse, the opposing team made fun of me as I ran. After a couple of laps, I had enough and slowed to a walk.

"Pick it up, Kurt. Get back to running," my coach yelled.

"No. I'm done. And if those other kids don't stop, I'm gonna kick their asses too."

Afterwards, the coach drove me home, then talked to my mother and her boyfriend, Chuck. I waited outside by the coach's car so I could get a head start when Chuck inevitably came for me.

Chuck was, by most accounts, a good guy. He was tall, approximately 6'4", with an athletic build. He had also spent time in prison so he had a badass side to him. Though he wasn't our step-father until much later in life, he often assumed a fatherly role when my brothers weren't jockeying for the position. Chuck wasn't the best person to look up to for many reasons, but he was the guy we had to answer to when shit went down.

Soon after hearing of my baseball performance, Chuck approached me with a deadly serious look in his eyes. "Kurky. Get your ass over here."

No way I was sticking around for this "conversation." I bolted from our house. Though he tried, Chuck couldn't catch me.

I returned home later that evening when Chuck was sleeping. We did have a talk the next morning but by then he had cooled off. Though I dodged a beating, I now had a bigger problem. Dismissed from the team and suspended from the league, I was left with a lot of free time on my hands.

Chapter Nine: Old Habits Die Hard

No longer able to play baseball, I could've used the opportunity to go to school and improve my life, but I didn't have much patience for that. I was living for the day and trying to survive as best I could.

It was a typical sunny South Florida morning in late May 1982. Summer was fast approaching and school would soon be ending. I was torn between prospects. On the one hand, I definitely enjoyed not having to worry about school: the tests, the homework, the obligation to ride in the dingy yellow school bus. On the other, I enjoyed going to school (when I did attend) because it meant free meals and a respite from the torment at home.

Though my memories of Juvie were still fresh, acting out was my lifestyle. It allowed me freedom and money to be independent. I rationalized my return to crime by attempting to limit my deeds. Here was my plan: I figured I could lessen any potential consequences by committing all my crimes in one day. If I was smart and careful, I could make enough cash to last me all summer long.

Deciding to skip school, I still walked to the bus stop located on the next street over from my house. Making sure my brothers and mother saw me heading in the right direction, I traveled beyond their eyesight, then ducked low behind a car, crouching to shield myself from detection. Reaching the end of the car, I stayed down, waiting for the bus to approach and leave. Once it was gone, I was in the safe zone and could quickly venture deeper into the neighborhood. As always, the key was to own my duplicity, looking and acting like I belonged here at this time of day.

My early morning consisted of little besides strolling around, enjoying my day off. I checked front porches and recycling bins for bottles to grab, but they were empty. As the day continued, hunger and boredom set in. I needed money, and the only way I knew to acquire it was by breaking into cars and homes.

I started at 10:00 AM, determined to smash my previous home burglary record. From piggy banks, to shoe boxes, to nightstands, and dresser drawers, I boosted my own personal savings. I broke into eight homes that day, all in my own neighborhood. My adrenaline soared as I moved from house to house like a professional, coolly popping out windows, removing screens, and discovering unlocked entrances. If I couldn't find an easy way in, I simply pivoted to the next house, thinking people were plain ignorant when it came to protecting their valuables.

As my victories continued, accumulating me more money, my appetite for something more grandiose began to eat at me. For the first time in my life, I took something other than cash.

When I was growing up, video game consoles had just been introduced. *Atari* was the first home game center I ever played, and I always envied my neighbors for owning one. We were so poor we could barely afford food. Needless to say, we wouldn't be purchasing our own *Atari* system anytime soon.

Rummaging through the eighth and final home that morning, I noticed the game console I had always wanted but could never afford. Like any kid on Christmas morning, I snatched my gift and didn't look back. The only problem was it wasn't mine to take. Not only that, I stupidly set it up at my house. *Big mistake.*

Though I considered myself smooth about getting in and out of houses without detection, my luck was about to change. Prior to today, I never thought anyone would notice stolen money. Instead, I figured my victims would just assume they misplaced it. However, this time, a homeowner definitely noticed the blank spot in the middle of their living room where their *Atari* used to sit. They called the police and filed a report. Meanwhile, another home reported the theft of several hundred dollars—I guess they *did* miss the money after all.

It didn't take the authorities long to realize the two robberies occurring in the same neighborhood were related. They ran fingerprints and found mine at the scene of the crimes. (Mine were now on file thanks to my last stint in Juvie.) Later that afternoon, a squad car pulled into our driveway and officers began questioning my mother.

Though the police confirmed they had my prints at the scene of the crime, I continued to deny wrongdoing. Problematically, I still had a wad of cash in my front pocket. The police, being keen observers, asked me what was in there.

"Nothing."

"Son, please empty your pockets now," demanded an officer.

Obliging, I did as I was told.

"Just because I have the money doesn't mean I stole it," I explained matter-of-factly.

The two cops looked at my mom and she stared at the money, seemingly uninterested.

"Ma'am, can we enter the house? We need to inspect for any other stolen property."

Don't do it mom, don't do it. Don't let them.

"Fine with me," my mother said.

Dammit! My stomach dropped. I could barely breathe as I trailed behind my mother and the two police officers. Walking into my room, they didn't even need to search—the *Atari* system sat there in the wide open.

Familiar cuffs slapped down on my wrists and I was thrown into another squad car. The doors slammed shut. From the window I watched my mother growing smaller and smaller as they drove me back to Juvie.

Chapter Ten: Juvie Surprises

The barbed wire gate shut behind me for the second time and immediately I thought of the Five. Marcus and the others had been tried and convicted for their crime against me, but still I worried about a chance encounter. Throughout the now familiar booking and intake process, I strategized what I might do if I ran into any of them again.

My worried thoughts were interrupted by the lovely "spread-your-cheeks-and-cough" examination, then I showered, and re-dressed myself in the standard-issue clothing. I got in line and awaited my instructions. *What Mod would they place me in this time?*

"Vari-chic-ee-oh," a guard called. "Where is Vari-chic-ee-oh?"

"Do you mean Varricchio?" I asked, annoyed.

"Is that how you say it? I ain't never seen a name like that. Are you him?"

"Yes. That's me."

"Okay. I need you to step out of line and stand over here to the side."

"Step where?"

"Over here—against the wall," the guard pointed.

"Why?"

"Because I said so. Boy, just do as I say and don't ask questions. You do that and we'll get along fine. Got it?"

"Yeah. I got it."

Removing myself from the line, I noticed other inmates' eyes on me. Although these weren't threatening stares like before, I didn't appreciate being the center of attention. This time around, I was determined to lay low and avoid confrontation with other inmates. I was not going to go through the same shit I did last time. Right out of the gate, however, I already stood apart from the crowd. *Damn. This is not how I wanted things to start.*

We were just about to leave when a black stocky female guard with short dark hair walked through the door. She pulled the intake guard aside to whisper something to him. As they spoke, the intake guard's eyes shifted to me and they nodded in agreement.

"Okay. I got him," she said, then walked toward me. "Hi, Kurt. I'm Officer Roundtree. You'll be coming with me."

"Okay," I said, not understanding why a female guard was escorting me. We left the intake area in the opposite direction of the male inmates. I clocked every landmark and room, trying to unravel my situation with each new clue. I noticed the cafeteria, then remembered one of the few highlights as an inmate—regular meal times. Then, we made an abrupt left turn. This was now uncharted territory.

After a few more feet, I noticed a large "G-1" on the front door to the Mod. *G-1? What does G-1 mean?* After a momentary memory lapse, I remembered exactly what "G-1" meant. The "G" stood for girls.

Guard Roundtree turned to me. "This is where you'll be staying."

"Sweet," I muttered to myself.

She scowled when she heard me. "I wouldn't get too comfortable. These girls aren't as kind as you might think. Watch yourself."

With that, the door to Mod G-1 opened and I entered what would be my new home.

Chapter Eleven: Acclimation

Life in the girl's Mod wasn't exactly a walk in the park, but during this stay at least I never had to worry about getting jumped by a group of thugs. Though placed with females during the day, I had to spend my evenings in an isolation cell located just outside the girl's Mod. Obviously, the authorities didn't want a 10-year-old male sleeping in the same area with fifteen to seventeen-year-old girls, even if, at the time, I thought it was a good idea.

I found my isolation cell to be pretty neat since I had the entire place to myself. I tried to personalize it by sticking pictures and posters to the wall with pieces of scotch tape I found around the detention center. The metal sink had just a large enough lip to hold a bar of soap, a small tube of toothpaste, and a toothbrush. I never had a bedroom to myself before, so this isolation cell was my sanctuary. It allowed me quiet time to contemplate things, from the cosmos to God. I even had time to dream, imagining far-out possibilities like becoming a famous movie star or a millionaire. Sometimes, I would dwell on my life's direction and what might happen to me as I grew older.

Often times, these lofty thoughts were interrupted by reality's harsh intrusion. The truth was I would never have the same opportunities as other kids my age because I was trapped. I had no role models, no real chances, and nobody watching over me. I was on my own. This was just the way things were and how they would always be. Or at least that's what I thought back then.

Sometimes these difficult realizations made me cry myself to sleep. Sadness morphed into anger when I considered life's unfairness. A ten-year-old boy should be playing baseball, joking with friends, having sleepovers— not sleeping on the streets, being forced to run away from home, and living in a juvenile detention center. For the first time, I started to think about things beyond the present moment. Maybe I was maturing, or maybe this was just what isolation did to people.

At first, I didn't pay much attention to the time passing. I figured I would be stuck in Juvie for a week, or two tops, but as the hours grew into days, I realized I was to be incarcerated for a longer haul. Accepting this fact, I worked hard to endear myself to the staff and guards. My outreach worked, and they gave me multiple job duties, considered to be an exceptional honor and privilege. For instance, mopping main hallway floors was one of the best jobs an inmate could have because it provided freedom from the craziness within the Mods. Such responsibility also offered a sense of worth and recognition and I relished the opportunity.

Often times, I would be cleaning a floor in the main halls and hear a call over the loudspeakers. "Attention! Attention!" the voice would say. "Code blue in Mod B-2. I repeat: a code blue in Mod B-2. All guards report immediately." I would drop my mop and sprint down the hall to the action.

Mod B-2 was for the big boys—sixteen and seventeen-year-olds, as well as some of the brawnier, brasher fifteen-year-olds. A "code blue" meant a fight was in progress.

Whenever I heard this happening, I knew the big boys were brawling. Usually I arrived at the tail-end only to see the repercussions on the participants' faces. Mod B-2 was known for nasty altercations because these boys were not only bigger and stronger but would gang up in groups of four or five to jump some hapless soul. I empathized with the victims' injuries, knowing I, too, would only end up the same way if I did much else but observe.

On one of my treks to the code blue battleground, I noticed some of the more intimidating inmates. There was one inmate in particular who seemed to be at the center of most, if not all, of the fights. Although he was not always active in the fracas, he called the shots. I quickly realized this boy was the *man* in charge. B-2 was his turf and he made sure others knew it, especially the newbies. Once I spied how he used his minions to carry out his objectives, I knew what I had to do next to finally secure my Juvie standing.

***

While floor cleaner was a great position, there was another, far more coveted job than mop patrol. This job ranked so high every inmate pursued it, yet very few received it. This role was Snack Duty.

The Juvie facility allocated three meals a day: breakfast, lunch, and dinner, as well as an evening snack around 7 or 8 pm. Every inmate looked forward to this snack as it typically included three cookies and a carton of milk or juice. Snacks became negotiation tools in exchange for extra dinner items, or a way to bet on sporting events and card games. In the ranks of juvenile delinquents, an evening snack became currency. The fact I now exerted some control over this influential mechanism provided opportunities and prestige.

In addition to receiving extra cookies and drinks in the evening, snack duty had another perk. Since I was in charge of the snack cart, I could move from Mod-to-Mod, hand-delivering goodies to the inmates. As a result, I was warmly received by others for essentially playing the role of Santa Claus, bearing gifts every night.

Quickly grasping the significance of this chance, I leveraged my new position to increase my rank amongst the inmates, not by trying to influence each and every inmate directly—*but by influencing the influencers*. The first kid I wanted to get onboard with my vision was the leader in Mod B-2, the man amongst boys running Mod B-2 like a boss—Jerome.

Jerome had commanded Mod B-2 for a while. Colossally built like an NFL linebacker, he even commanded the respect of the guards. The scant number of inmates who didn't respect Jerome still feared him like a predatory shark. This combination fueled his rise up the Juvie food chain. Everyone swimming below him cowered in his wake, doing all they could do for him so they wouldn't become his evening snack. Even the guards respected Jerome's strength and bigger-than-life presence.

A week into serving at my new post, I approached Jerome with the snack cart. I tried to hold it steady. I didn't want my nerves to betray me. As I drew closer to his cell, I locked my hands down on the U-shaped metal bar and slid it smoothly to a stop. *So far, so good.*

"Here you go, buddy." I politely handed him a milk carton and an evening snack rolled into a napkin. "Enjoy your evening."

I strolled away to the next cell, keeping an eye out to see if he noticed my kind gesture. Inside the napkin were six cookies, double the standard allotment. This act let him know I was looking out for him, taking care of him by giving him privileges no other inmate received. Upon opening the napkin and discovering the additional cookies he turned and gave me a head nod.

"Thanks, little man," he said.

"No problem. I got your back," I whispered. "Just keep it between us."

After that, I continued my Mod rounds, knowing step one was in place.

For the next week, I continued the same procedure, giving Jerome extra snacks every night, and, whenever possible, an extra drink or two. I sought to establish a relationship, knowing if I could befriend the most feared and respected inmate, it would make my life easier inside this place.

"Here you go, Jerome," I would say. "Your standard."

"Thanks, man. Appreciate you doing that."

Then, one day, our relationship took a big step forward, allowing me to accomplish step two. After giving Jerome his standard double-snack, he placed his big paw of a hand on my shoulder, his arm resting across the back of my neck. "If you ever need anything in here, little man, you let me know," he said. "I mean, if anyone messes with you or anything, you let me know and I'll take care of it."

"Thanks, man." I suppressed my pulsing adrenaline to manage a smile. "I appreciate that."

He released me and I went back to my cart. As I continued distributing smaller snacks to the other inmates, my confidence grew tenfold. I was ecstatic. The biggest, baddest dude in all of Juvie was now in my corner. I now had serious backup if anyone tried anything with me.

Soon after that exchange, I became Jerome's confidante. We would often talk in the cafeteria during meals, in the yard during recreation time, and whenever we saw each other. To be honest, I let *him* do most of the talking so he would feel comfortable sharing more and more each time. When you do nothing but listen, it's amazing how much more people share with you. He told me about his life outside Juvie, his family, how many girlfriends he had, and whatever else was on his mind. Such comradery increased my confidence level, helping me feel certain he would protect me if ever needed.

Our walk-and-talks occurred all over the institution. Sometimes it was just a "what's up", but no matter how deep the conversation, I made sure everyone else noticed our exchanges. Public knowledge of our friendship was crucial to my protection. The closer we became, the higher my survival chances. This relationship saved me a lot of issues, I am sure, but for one unfortunate nitwit who never received the memo.

Chapter Twelve: Calling in the Guns

"Take care, little man. I'll see you later tonight."

It was just after dinner and all around the cafeteria, kids were getting up to leave. Jerome gave me the universal head nod, then left the cafeteria with the rest of the Mod B-2 big boys.

As soon as they left, some punk from Mod B-1 started in with me.

"*See you later tonight,*" he quipped, puckering his lips into a kissing shape. "What are you? His little butt buddy?"

Even though this boy was bigger than me, I responded like I usually did to stupid jerks. "Go fuck yourself."

He didn't appreciate that. "What'd you say? Come say that to my face, you little prick."

Knowing I had the protection of Juvie's toughest inmate, I stood my ground. "You heard me. I said, 'go fuck yourself.'"

"That's it, you little shit!"

He gripped a plastic chair, screeching it across the floor as he glanced toward the guards. His face angrily contorted. It looked like not being able to throw the chair physically pained him. "Your ass is mine."

I smirked. He didn't like that reaction either.

"I'm going to kick your ass. Better hope there are guards by your side at all times."

I laughed in his face, only fueling a tirade. He called me every dirty name he could possibly think of.

When he was done, I said, "You don't know who you're messing with, punk. I'd pipe down if I were you."

He lost his cool and lunged at me. Before he could reach me, two guards firmly planted their hands on his chest.

"You're lucky they're here." He practically foamed at the mouth. "'Cause I'm gonna kick the ever livin' shit out of you when I get my chance."

"Whatever. We'll see."

Uttering those last words, I walked away. That evening, I made my standard snack run. By the time I reached the punk, I thought he would've calmed down. I was wrong. He was playing a game of cards with another inmate and began chiding me as soon as I set down their snacks.

"Where's your little butt buddy?" he asked in the same mocking tone. "Is he waiting in his cell for you?"

"I'm sure you'll have a chance to meet him soon enough if you keep this shit up. You need to shut up before you get yourself in a bad place."

"Why don't you make me shut up, pussy?"

Now he was pissing me off. Though he was bigger, I thought about throwing a haymaker and getting in at least one good shot before he got to me. No doubt I could land a solid punch, but if I went this route, there were two strong possibilities. First, I would lose my snack duty patrol, and with that, the small amount of control that came with it. Second, a good chance existed this bigger kid would get in a few shots before the guards arrived. Neither of these options seemed too enticing so I pressed on with my cart.

"Yeah, looks like you're scared without your boyfriend 'round, little pussy."

Stopping, I realized he wanted me to swing first—still, I held back. The last time I let my temper get the better of me, they threw me off the baseball team. There were bigger stakes involved now. If I swung first, I'd be punished first. As a juvenile delinquent, my ability to survive required me to recognize others' manipulation tactics. I'm not saying everyone should get in trouble with the law to better understand psychology but being in the system had sharpened my empathic abilities. I knew what this guy was thinking and how to use it to my advantage. Though it bothered me to back down, I pressed on. Then I made eye contact with one of the guards, nodding toward the punk.

"Hey Kurt." The guard approached. "There a problem?"

"Yeah, there is." I quickly conjured up a white lie. "This kid keeps threatening to 'kick my ass' because I won't give him more snacks."

The punk shrank back in rage. "That's not true. He's lying!"

"Bullshit. You've been badgering me ever since I walked in here with the snack cart. I'm just trying to do my job. I don't need this crap."

Then I turned to the guard, asking innocently as I could, "I'm not allowed to give out any additional snacks, right? Even if someone threatens violence against me?"

"That's right," said the guard. He turned to the punk with a scowl. "You need to exit this area and leave Kurt alone or you'll find yourself in solitary."

The punk looked like his head might explode. "But that's not true. He's lying. I didn't threaten him."

"Yes, you did," I said.

"Enough," the guard yelled, directing us in opposite directions. "You go that way and you go that way."

Our exchange over, I continued through the Mod, handing out the rest of the snacks. As I took one more backward glance at the punk, he mouthed the words, "I'm going to kick your ass."

Being the smartass I was, I mouthed back, "No, you won't. Watch your back." Then I smiled at him, angering him more.

Up next for me was Mod B-2 and my boy, Jerome. I always took a little extra time handing out snacks in B-2 because I wanted to make sure the biggest, baddest kids in Juvie knew who I was. After all, if I built a relationship with them, chances were good I wouldn't have to encounter one of them in the wrong circumstances. Not only that, I knew Jerome would eventually leave Juvie so I needed contingency plans.

I spent a few extra minutes with Jerome that night explaining what transpired with the punk in Mod B-1.

"All right," Jerome said. "We'll take care of it."

"Thanks." I handed Jerome his extra snacks and drinks.

The following evening, I saw Jerome in the cafeteria at dinner with his regular posse. He gestured for me to come over and I approached with my tray of mystery meat and corn mush. He put his big paw on my shoulder, again pulling me in firmly. I gripped my tray so I wouldn't spill food in his lap.

"It's all taken care of, little man," he said, matter-of-factly. "He won't give you any more trouble."

I sighed with relief. "Thanks, man. I appreciate you having my back."

"No problem. You know we good."

As we exchanged the show of back-slapping affection reserved for times like these, I took an inventory of his clique at the table. All of their eyes had shifted to us. There were a couple of head nods—in civilian translation, that meant, 'I know who you are, and I'm aware of your pecking order in this juvenile detention center.' Though I was young and small, I knew confidence sold anything so I puffed up my chest, nodding to the whole table. Translation: 'Y'all got some extra cookies coming your way tonight.'

Returning to my side of the cafeteria, I saw him.

The punk's face was swollen and he had cuts up and down his forehead. A nasty black eye made it look like he just collided with a truck. He stumbled through the food line with a noticeable limp. I was proud my plan worked to perfection and my confidence soared. I had gone from a defenseless little kid to possessing the support of the toughest kids in Juvie and everyone knew it.

I don't know if Jerome did the deed himself or called in the order, but I needed to make sure this punk knew who was ultimately responsible. Once he sat down with his food, I stared at him until he felt it. When he turned around, we made eye contact. I scowled as I gave a head nod. Translation: 'Don't mess with me anymore.'

He simply looked down at his plate in silence. He never messed with me again.

Chapter Thirteen: A Rose by Any Other Name

Though Jerome had my back when interacting with males, he couldn't save me from interactions with the Juvie females. As mentioned, I was incarcerated in the girls' Mod. During the day, I stayed in the general population area with the girls, excluding the times I was placed in the yard with males or during various other activities. At night, I went to my isolation cell.

I relished my time with the female inmates. Most of them were aged fifteen to seventeen-years old, so they were like my older sisters. A few actually watched over me, making sure I didn't step out of line. One girl in particular, Stacie, took on the most protective role toward me.

Sixteen-years-old, Stacie had long, sandy blonde hair she kept in a ponytail, stood 5'9" and had a little extra meat on her. She wasn't severely overweight, but she did have big bones and girth, making her look tough. I have no doubt she could've kicked the snot out of half the boys in Mod B-1 and would put up a good fight against the others.

I spent a lot of time playing cards and dominoes with Stacie in the back of the Mod. When it was time to leave, she always made sure I was at the front of the line. If I wasn't near her, I'd hear, "Where's Kurt?"

"I'm here," I would yell to Stacie from the back of the line.

"Well, get your little ass up here, boy," she would demand, and I'd make my way to the front.

If I ever lagged too long or didn't respond when she first yelled, Stacie would admonish me. I'm not sure if the other girls appreciated the attention I got or not, but like Jerome, Stacie ran her Mod and nobody questioned her.

There's an important difference between confidence and cockiness, especially when it comes to being in Juvie. The latter can lead to big problems. One afternoon in the Girls Mod, I got cocky.

One day, some guards had summoned me to watch a drama production in the rec room. This was a large area used by all the inmates for many activities, like movie screenings and concerts. It was also where they brought in entertainers or guest speakers to perform or speak to the kids. On those occasions, I would usually find Jerome and his crew to sit by them. There was no sense trying to become friends with anyone else when I had the ear of Jerome and his group.

I don't recall the performance that afternoon, but I do vividly recall what happened afterward. As I was escorted back to the Girls Mod I was in some kind of silly mood—feeling overconfident. Approaching the Mod, I noticed the girls sitting in a group watching a show.

The guard opened the door, and I walked in. Then I made the mistake of opening my mouth. "What's up, bitches?" I yelled, holding my crotch. "Yeah, yeah. What's up, bitches?"

Naturally, all of the girls looked at me. Some of them laughed and smiled, but others pursed their lips in a solid line, definitely unamused. I continued holding my crotch like a total punk. I don't know what got into me, but it landed me in trouble very quickly.

"What'd you say?" asked Rose, a tough new inmate.

"You heard me. I said, WHAT'S UP, BITCHES?"

"I know you ain't calling me a bitch."

"Yeah, I'm calling you a bitch, BITCH," I replied, still holding my crotch, but this time pulling on it as if to offer it to her. "You know you want this, girl. Yes, you KNOW it."

"You better check yourself, little punk," she sternly replied. "Or I'll come knock the white off you."

Rose was a sixteen-year-old black girl with cornrows and a wiry frame. She had been incarcerated before and wasn't about to listen to some ten-year-old white boy disrespect her, especially in front of other inmates. On the other hand, I wasn't going to allow a new inmate to question my position in Juvie either, especially not a girl, so I opened my big mouth again, escalating tensions.

"Bitch, I'd like to see you come over here and try something, you skanky ass ho," I stupidly replied.

With that, Rose was on her way over—in a hurry. By now, I had been in my fair share of fights, scrapping with my share of boys—but the fire in Rose's eyes had me shitting in my pants. I was about to get turned inside out. I started running and she chased me. I jumped over a chair and she leaped after me. I ran toward the back of the Mod and she trailed like a cheetah hunting an antelope on the Serengeti. *This girl was fast.* I maneuvered around a couple of tables, then double-backed toward the seating area with Rose still hot on my heels.

As I was charging through the fray, jumping over inmates, I heard a loud *whack* behind me. It sounded like the collision of two linebackers. As I turned to see what happened, I noticed Rose and Stacie in an all-out brawl. They pulled hair and punches flew before they knocked each other to the ground in a bloody tussle.

"Holy shit," I yelled. "Kick her ass, Stacie."

Guards suddenly swarmed in to break up the fight. Both girls looked equally messed up as they were dragged kicking and screaming to isolation. Rose was first to go. She delivered a few choice words to me before being pulled away.

"I'm coming for your ass," she threatened. "Don't worry, boy—I'm gonna getchya." She smiled through bloody teeth. "Believe that! Believe that!"

I simply smirked back at her. "Yeah, yeah."

Right after Rose, Stacie was escorted toward the front.

"Thanks, Stacie," I sheepishly said as she walked by. "I'm sorry."

"No worries," she said. "Nobody messes with my little brother. I'll be back soon." Then she gestured to her clique. "You girls look after him 'til I get back."

"You got it, Stacie," one replied.

"Yeah, we got him." said another.

Once Stacie was gone, another girl called to me. "Get over here, boy."

I quickly joined the group. In a matter of minutes, we were playing cards and rehashing the details of the fight. Things were back to normal—or at least what's normal in juvenile hall.

Chapter Fourteen: Isolated

"Wake up." A guard knocked on the shatterproof glass window of my isolation cell door. "Time to get moving. Breakfast in twenty."

In a daze, I stumbled to the toilet three feet away. After using it, I splashed cold water on my face, then groggily brushed my teeth. I sat back on my bed, waiting for a guard to open the door and take me to the cafeteria. Today I was thinking about life more than usual. I considered my situation, the situation my brothers were in, the situation my mother was in, and what life might be like if so many things were different. The more I pondered, the sadder I got. Today was my 11th birthday and I couldn't even open my own door to walk outside.

When most kids turn eleven, they celebrate with their family and friends. After all, this is the foray into the "real" double-digits—the big time. I had never had a birthday party before. The only thing remotely close was the time I attended a friend's birthday at McDonald's. I tried to imagine how cool it would be to have my own party. Unfortunately, there was no chance of that happening. What made matters even worse was nobody cared. Nobody would be wishing me "happy birthday" today.

Of course, part of the reason why nobody wished me a happy birthday was because no one knew it was my birthday. Though I was more outspoken and now carried myself confidently in Juvie, I avoided telling personal things to other inmates they could use to their advantage.

After a long day, I returned to my isolation cell around 10:00 p.m. Staring up at the ceiling, far from the others, my tears began to fall. I thought about how bad of a place I was in on this special day—not just a bad place physically, but a bad place emotionally and spiritually. I was truly alone.

My birthday came and went, and nobody cared. Inching toward the edge of despair, I had wild, desperate thoughts. *What if I just disappeared? Would anyone care? Would anyone even notice?*

Wrapping the covers over my head, I resolved to go to sleep. Then I heard a knock.

"Kurt," someone whispered. There was a tap on the glass. "You up?"

I wasn't expecting anybody, especially not at this hour. "Yeah, I'm here," I replied cautiously. "Who is it?"

I used the bed sheet to dry my face.

"It's Vernon."

Vernon was one of my favorite guards in Juvie. A kindhearted, older black gentleman in his mid-50s, he looked after the inmates' welfare. He usually worked the graveyard shift, and though he had worked in the system for a while, he didn't do it for money. He wanted to help juvenile delinquents—pure and simple. He took an interest in us, engaging in our interests, seeking ways to improve our lives.

In many ways, Vernon was the closest thing us kids had in the way of a father figure. He wasn't interested in beating kids down emotionally, but rather lifting them up through positive thinking. It seemed like all we ever heard as juvenile delinquents was how shitty we were, how we were nothing but screw-ups who would never amount to anything. Most of us were written off by the system before we were even twelve-years-old. Some kids, myself included, were labeled unredeemable even earlier than that.

Vernon, however, didn't believe in those kinds of labels. He didn't believe in giving up on kids. Every child in Juvie possessed something special, he thought, and it just sometimes took longer to determine what that special quality was. Vernon never directly blamed us for our plight. Instead, he tried to make us understand we had a tougher mountain to climb because of circumstances beyond our control. He always challenged us to think bigger—beyond the moment. He encouraged us to find new ways of dealing with anxiety and socio-economic inequality. I will always remember him as someone who genuinely made an impact.

Knowing it was Vernon outside my door, I relaxed. "What's up, Vernon?"

"Well, I heard it was somebody's birthday today," he said through shatterproof glass. "So I wanted to see if you have time to celebrate."

What? He heard it was my birthday? He wants to celebrate?

I sprang out of bed. "Yeah, it's my birthday." I walked right up to the door. "How'd you know?"

"Hey, buddy." He smiled. "It's my job to know."

Looking back, I'm not surprised Vernon kept track of these things. He always went the extra mile to understand us. His is a philosophy I try to use now. Breaking through to another person can be as simple as seeing them.

Vernon opened my cell and I immediately noticed a bag in his hand. "Now, let's have a little celebration," he said. "This is the big one-one."

Escorting me from my cell, he brought me to a separate room used for meetings with counselors and attorneys. Vernon opened his bag, handing me candy bars and soda. "I know it's late and this might keep you up all night, but what the heck?"

"Sounds good to me!"

Vernon and I played cards for hours, chatting about everything, from my favorite sports heroes to what I could improve upon in juvenile hall.

"I heard you created a stir in the girls' Mod." He flipped over his cards to show a pair of Jacks.

"Yeah," I admitted, displaying my nothing-hand.

"All that crotch grabbing stuff—it's time to grow out of that stage. You need to be more respectful to the female inmates."

"Okay." I never wanted to disappoint Vernon. "I'm going to do better."

Two hours into our playing and chatting, Vernon revealed another surprise. "I got something else for you. It's not much, but you can't really have much in here anyways."

He handed me a couple of small gifts wrapped in colorful wrapping paper. "Happy Birthday, Kurt."

A huge smile spread across my face. "Thank you, Vernon."

Once I opened his gifts, which included playing cards and some smaller games to keep me busy in isolation, he mentioned he had one last thing to share with me. "What would a birthday celebration be without a cake?"

He placed a small, chocolate cake on the table with the words "Happy Birthday" written in frosting across the top. Since lighting a flame in Juvie was against the rules, I pretended to blow out the candles after he sang *Happy Birthday.* We played cards until 2 a.m. that night. Between the sugar high and the emotional boost from Vernon's kindness, it took me an hour to finally drift to sleep. The day had taken a positive turn at just the right time and I was very grateful.

Chapter Fifteen: Muted Fireworks

In Juvie, if you are at the bottom of the food chain, there is only one way up and that's to fight. If you don't, get ready for pain: constant ridicule, beatings, even rape. I understood this reality all too well. My only hope for survival often meant battling thirteen-years-olds and below. I had little or no problem handling kids under this age and considered it, by and large, a fair matchup, though I was usually much smaller than my adversaries. Problems arose, though, whenever another eleven or twelve-year-old landed in Juvie. Younger kids always wanted to assert their dominance in the pecking order.

There were two other young boys who arrived after I had already established my reputation in the hierarchy. One of these, Lionel Washington, was eleven. The other, DeAndre Jackson, was twelve. Initially, Lionel, DeAndre, and I stuck together and became good friends. We watched each other's backs and made sure to hang in the yard during rec times or in the rec room when we could all be together.

Eventually, however, Lionel and DeAndre both took issue with my status in Juvie and things started to change. The transformation occurred gradually. There were little things: occasional grumblings from DeAndre and Lionel, questioning why I was more highly regarded by other inmates and the guards. Then they started begrudging me for landing the more coveted jobs. Jealousy set in and battle lines were drawn.

"How come you got snack duty, cleaning the floors, and all that shit?" DeAndre asked me one day as we were shooting baskets in the yard.

"I busted my ass, man," I said.

"Seems like you're the favorite around here." He took a shot that crashed off the backboard.

"Yeah," Lionel chimed in with his usual one-word comments.

"You seem pretty highly fucking regarded," DeAndre continued, taunting.

"I'm just trying to protect myself. I worked for it." I was getting annoyed they were trying to knock me off my perch.

As more awkward conversations like this continued, I readied myself for war. But on the surface, I proceeded as if nothing was wrong. I heard rumbles of Lionel and DeAndre's grievances against me to our B-1 peers. These two were at the bottom of the pecking order and didn't like it. The fact I spent an inordinate amount of time with the girls also set their jealousies aflame.

One night, things came to a head. Making my usual snack run, I entered B-1. Suddenly, Lionel and DeAndre approached with a group of inmates trailing behind. This was unusual, but I tried to play it off.

"What's up, guys? Here's your snacks." I handed them an extra cookie or two and proceeded with general distribution.

The group, led by DeAndre, followed after me.

"Say something, DeAndre," I heard one inmate mumble.

"Yeah, DeAndre," chimed in another. "Let him know what's up."

Let me know what's up?

"I don't like how you think you run shit 'round here, man," DeAndre chirped. "And I think things gonna change."

It irked me he was challenging me in front of everyone but I tried not to show my irritation. "What the hell you talking about? We're cool, right?"

"Nah, we ain't cool."

Now I was growing pissed. "You're trippin', man. You're listening to too many people—we're good."

"Nah, nigga, we ain't."

Before I could get another word in, DeAndre threw a haymaker, hitting me on the side of the head.

"What the fuck, DeAndre?"

Continuing with profanities, I threw my own haymakers. We tackled each other to the ground and started brawling. The guards quickly ran over to break us up, but we continued to go at it.

"Calm down, boys," one guard yelled.

Even after the guards pulled us off one another, we didn't stop. I took off my shoes and threw them at DeAndre's face. "I will fuck you up, DeAndre!"

There was no giving up from either one of us—we knew what was at stake. The guards restrained us as we continued to scream at each other, struggling to get loose to fight more. That evening, both of us were placed in isolation cells to "reflect upon our actions." Since some guards got caught in our crossfire, we were required to spend multiple days "reflecting."

One of these days was the 4th of July, where this story first began. The Ft. Lauderdale Juvenile Detention Center was located just off Broward Boulevard, west of I-95, approximately five miles from world-famous beaches. Every Independence Day, the city coordinated a huge fireworks display, lighting up the South Florida sky. It was a spectacular event, especially for little kids to marvel at awe-inspiring, colorful explosions accentuated by thunderous booms.

They shut the lights off in my cell around 9:00 pm. As I lay in bed staring at the ceiling, I wondered if I could see the fireworks so I lifted myself to take a look. There they were! Although I was a good distance from the launch site, I could still see the display from my cell. All the colors of the rainbow blasted through the distant sky. It was spectacular, but for one missing element. There were no accompanying booms or crackles and no stirring music accompanying the choreographed explosions.

As the fireworks continued to launch, I kept watching, but my excitement ebbed. For the first time in my life, I truly felt the effects of my incarceration. To me, this was worse than watching television without the sound because it was real life unfolding. I knew thousands of people were out there enjoying the total 4th of July experience, meanwhile, I was confined to a tiny cell with thick, shatter-proof (and sound-proof) windows.

My wonderment melted to sadness. The fact was, the world was going on without me and nobody gave a shit whether I was on the ride or not. In this moment, I realized I had to make an adjustment. I wanted to be a part of the celebrations. I wanted to be more than a number. *I wanted to matter.* Though I wouldn't change overnight, I credit this self-reflective moment for the dramatic changes that would one day come.

Chapter Sixteen: So Long, Sisters

"Varricchio," the stocky guard named Roundtree shouted.

I picked up my cards to play *Spades* with a few girls in the Mod again.

"*Varricchio*," she yelled louder.

"Yeah," I said, annoyed at the interruption. "I'm here." I waved my hand in the air.

"Get your stuff," she said. "It's time for you to go."

"Go?" I asked, now interested. "What are you talking about?"

"It's time for you to go," she said again, as if I should've known this already. "Time for you to leave Juvie."

"Holy crap!" I jumped up from my seat. "Are you serious? I'm getting out of this place? *Finally?*"

I turned to the girls at the table. "I'm out of here, girls. I'm going home."

I high-fived them, my excitement growing. Roundtree, however, quickly tempered my joy. "No. You're not going home, Varricchio. You're going to a group home."

"A what?"

"You'll find out soon enough. Get your stuff."

I turned to the girls. "What the hell is a group home?"

"It's a place where you live with other kids like you," one of them explained. "Basically, you'll live in a real house with other messed up kids."

"It's better than Juvie, but it ain't home," another girl added.

"You'll be all right, Kurty," another chimed in. "It beats this place."

"That's true," the first girl said, picking up my hand of cards and shuffling them back into the deck. "Much better than this crappy shit."

Although I knew they were probably right, I was going to miss them. For the last two-and-a-half months, I had spent most of my waking hours with these girls. They became my confidants, my friends and, in a twisted way, my family. Aside from the Rose situation, which was entirely my fault, these girls never tried to harm me. A rare feeling of safety was about to be ripped from me. I knew I couldn't stay in the Girls Mod forever, but I still felt stung at hearing news of my relocation.

The best way to communicate in Juvie was not through words, but via body language, so I said my goodbyes through silent exchanges: shaking hands, exchanging high-fives, giving all-knowing head nods. But when I found my way to Stacie, sitting in her usual spot in front of the television, I knew a small, physical gesture wouldn't be enough. "Well, Stacie," I started. "I guess it's time—"

"Shut up and get over here. Give me a hug, you little shit."

Stacie and I embraced despite the facility's rule forbidding inmates from engaging in physical contact.

"Are we allowed to hug?" I asked Stacie as she squeezed the air out of me.

"Fuck 'em. I gotta hug my little brother."

Stacie was tough as they came, but I knew my leaving impacted her, especially since it happened so quickly. I was also having a hard time with the realization I may never see her again. Although she didn't cry, she was choked up as we ended our embrace. "You listen to me," she instructed me, looking me in the eyes while holding both my shoulders. "You take care of yourself and watch your back. Don't ever let your guard down."

She looked like she wanted to say something else, but the words wouldn't come so she pulled me back in for another hug. "I don't know if we'll ever see each other again, but I'll be thinking of you."

All of a sudden, she pulled herself away and patted me on the head. "Okay, get your little ass out of here," she said, then quickly returned to her chair. The atmosphere in the Mod felt awkward and depressing. Stacie only showed emotions when someone crossed her. Now that she was exhibiting vulnerability, she quickly put an end to it. "Who the hell put this crap on television?" she yelled. "Garbage!"

She faced the television but I could see her looking at me from the corner of her eye as I approached the exit. With the guard's hand on my arm, I took one last look behind me. Stacie's eyes looked a little misty, but she continued to stare at the screen. When another girl came up to Stacie to put her arm around her, Stacie quickly dislodged it.

"I'm good," she insisted. "Just change the fucking channel."

With that, I left the Mod for the very last time, never to see Stacie again.

Chapter Seventeen: Group Home

I was grateful this social worker didn't like small talk. A four-hour trip in a state-issued vehicle is one I wanted to spend in silence. They put me in the first row of the back of the van. I looked down and saw my name at the top of the driver's sheet as we continued north on I-95. I stared at the five-digit case number wondering who was #1, and if any of the thousands before me had been to this same group home. *Did they make it out alive? Did they return to Juvie?* Part of me wanted to rip that paper to shreds, leap from the vehicle, and break into a nice home—not to steal anything—but just to take a long nap. Afterwards, it wouldn't be too bad to play some Atari and eat junk food until I fell back asleep.

The car hit a bump. I shook my head, knowing fantasies could be dangerous. I needed to devote my thoughts to survival strategies at my new group home in Holly Hill, Florida. Located in Volusia County, just north of Daytona Beach, this area was best known for the *Daytona 500*. As we pulled into a long, compact dirt road, I wondered if these new people might take me to the speedway one day. I stopped myself again. The less expectations, the less disappointment.

We continued for about 500 feet before coming upon a large, ranch-style home. The first thing I noticed were farm animals. *What the heck?* I noted a pony, a pig, and a number of chickens and roosters running around the gated area. I wasn't sure if I should be concerned or excited, so I landed on reserved acceptance. The social worker got out of the car first to talk to an older woman on the front porch. He handed her my paperwork and left as I walked up, kicking up dust.

"Well, hello there," Hanna said with a huge grin.

Probably in her late 40's or early 50's, Hanna looked every bit maternal. Patches of gray streaked her dark, straight hair. She wore glasses and was a little heavy, although not too overweight. Her build reflected both her blue-collar work ethic and motherly temperament. No doubt she could go out to the chicken coop to gather eggs in the morning, then cook a solid meal for breakfast, all the while coaching kids on the importance of proper manners.

"We've been expecting you." She grabbed my hands. "How was your ride here?"

I wasn't sure how to react to this overly excited woman so I shrugged. "It was okay."

"Great. That's great. Rudy! He's here, come out here." She turned her attention back toward me. "You're going to meet my husband, Rudy. He's a great guy—you'll love him. All the kids do."

Rudy came out and shook my hand. "Hi there, Kurt. So happy to have you join us."

Ever the blue-collar guy too, Rudy was nearly six feet and heavy, though he carried the weight well. He must've been in his early 50s and had seen many long days of hard labor. He looked like the kind of handy guy who could fix anything at any time.

"Hi," I said, trying to reciprocate Rudy's firm handshake.

"We've been waiting for you to get here because we have a special event tonight. Did you tell him, dear?" he asked Hanna.

"Not yet. He literally just walked in the door," Hannah replied, barely able to hide her own excitement. "Well, Kurt. We are going to see a movie tonight."

Go to a movie? I had been to a theater just twice in my entire life. Once to see the film *Convoy* and the other time to see *Stir Crazy*. Of course, I was not sure why my mom took me to see the latter R-rated feature when I was just nine-years-old, but I thought it was hilarious. Soon after giving me the good news about the movie trip, I was introduced to the other group-home kids. In total, there were seven of us and we all carried different emotional baggage. As we hopped into the van, they wanted to figure out mine.

"What's your name?" a boy with shaggy blonde hair asked.

"Kurt," I said, looking around at the sea of faces.

A boy in the back tugged at my ear. I whipped around, ready for confrontation, then softened as he slumped back in his seat. "Where you from?"

"Fort Lauderdale Juvie," I said, turning back, my defenses lowering.

"How'd you end up there?" a boy in a grey skull t-shirt asked. "I stole a million dollars. What'd you do?"

Hanna looked at me from the front passenger seat. "You may have some exaggerators in your midst."

"Could've been a million," he muttered. "Got caught though."

"Broke into some cars and homes," I confidently replied so as to establish credibility out the gate. They all nodded, understanding.

"Almost got an *Atari*," I said triumphantly.

A chorus of "oohs" and "ahhs" ripped through the van. Hanna told us to please quiet down. I leaned toward the back seat and whispered, "How's the house? The farm?"

The boy in the skull shirt shrugged. "Better than jail. But the roosters are so loud. It's like a train running into your house every morning. And they smell."

"Don't listen to him," an older boy said, popping gum. "You'll see for yourself." He turned to the kid in the skull shirt. "And stop exaggerating."

"I never exaggerate!"

I turned back around, relieved I hadn't made any enemies—yet.

That night, we saw *E.T. the Extra-Terrestrial*. I sat at the end of the row, which was actually a good thing, because at the end of the movie, I cried a little. Of course, I didn't want anyone to see me as being "soft" so I made sure I turned my head away from the screen. I'm not sure what got into me that evening, but there was something about E.T having to leave his new best friend, Elliot, behind while he returned "home." Maybe it was that final exchange I had with Stacie earlier or perhaps the fact I didn't have a best friend, but I was overcome with emotion and struggled to keep things in check at the theater. *What a wuss. Crying over a stupid movie.*

Later that evening, we returned to the group home. I stayed in a room in the back of the house with two bunk beds. It had its own bathroom, but I was still concerned about being with the largest number of kids. Incidentally, I was, once again, the youngest one in the facility, so I knew I would have to establish my ground rules in due time. Tonight, however, wasn't the right moment, so I simply jumped into the top bunk, pulled the covers up tightly to my neck and drifted off to sleep, thinking about what tomorrow would bring.

Chapter Eighteen: Baseball and Deep Thoughts

Rudy gave me another chance at baseball. Behind the house was a large field where we scrimmaged on a daily basis. No more catchers to bully me. No more strikes on every swing. During the summer, we played our hearts out, competing with other neighborhood kids. Naturally, it was "Rudy and Hanna's Boys" versus the other children.

I really enjoyed playing against our rivals for two big reasons. First, because we were juvenile delinquents, the other kids didn't think we could play. I guess they thought we spent more time incarcerated than on the diamond, which was actually a valid assessment. This smug attitude, however, fueled my fire to prove them wrong.

Second, playing against the neighborhood kids gave us the opportunity to work as a team. We learned how to coordinate to achieve the ultimate goal—victory. Although we had our differences and engaged in our share of fights, we came together on the field for a common goal. Often times, the euphoria of securing a victory could even carry us through several days of peace amongst each other. I knew Rudy saw the value in this and I'm sure that's why he spent his own money buying us gear and equipment.

Some afternoons, Rudy came outside to watch us play. He worked at his lawn business during the day, but if he ever finished his route early, he would step in as umpire and cheerleader. Rudy knew a lot about baseball and always had pointers for us, both during and after the game.

"Why would you throw the ball to third base, Ronnie?" Rudy would yell from behind the plate. "You have two outs. Just get the last out at first base."

One day I was playing centerfield with a runner on second. My team was up by two runs and we had two outs. The ball shot towards me on a line drive. I charged at it, secured it in my glove, then came up throwing as hard as I could to home plate to nail the runner who tried to score from second base. My throw sailed over the catcher's head, allowing the batter to reach third. (Because we had no backstop, we created a rule allowing only two bases for an overthrow to home plate; otherwise, the batter could easily score as the ball rolled under the fence and into the horse's stable.)

"Kurt," Rudy yelled, more to be heard rather than to scold me. "Why would you do that now?"

"I wanted to throw him out, Rudy. Isn't that the goal?"

"Not at this time in the game, it isn't." He walked to the pitcher's mound, talking to us much like a coach would. "Everybody hold on a second."

All the kids gathered around him, panting from their efforts.

"Listen," Rudy said. "You're up by two runs with two outs in the last inning. And you have a runner on base who isn't as important as the guy at the plate."

I wasn't sure I agreed with Rudy at this point, so I spoke up. "What do you mean he's not important? If he scores, then we are only up one run."

"Yes, but you are *still up one run* and you only need one out. The guy you need to keep from scoring is him." Rudy pointed to the batter standing on third. "Now, you have the tying run at third base, rather than first base."

"But he's still on base, Rudy, and he can still score from first," said another kid.

"Yes, but there are so many more things that could happen in a positive way for you defensively if the kid is still at first," Rudy explained. "Rather than try to make a great play with a runner who doesn't mean much, you should *minimize* your risk by keeping this guy, the batter, as far from home plate as possible. That means, Kurt, you need to simply throw the ball to second and allow the run to score."

The reasoning behind "minimizing the risk" stuck with me. This concept is akin to keeping a molehill from growing into a mountain. Or letting a punk talk shit to you in B-1, knowing losing face is okay short-term until you can do something about it. Ultimately, when something isn't going right, it's best to consider all options as dispassionately as possible. Consider the safest, most efficient approach in light of a setback. Although you may only win by one run instead of two, you can still triumph by addressing the adverse situation with an eye towards minimizing risk. Taking the safest approach in the face of adversity, however, is difficult, especially for adolescents. As I knew all too well from my confrontation with DeAndre and Lionel, a major obstacle for evaluating options in stressful situations is our own emotional responses, including stubbornness. When throwing that ball to home plate, I wanted to nail the runner because I thought it was important to keep our lead and win by two runs. I also wanted to look like the hero by gunning the kid at the plate. I didn't even think that keeping the batter at first base was important. As long as I threw out the runner at home plate, I could've cared less about that other runner because it would have been our third out; the game would've been over and I would've been the hero.

In this line of reasoning, I failed to consider the consequences of not throwing out the runner at home plate. I was so wrapped up in the potentially positive outcome (ending the game), I forgot to consider the ramifications (both positive and negative) of my actions. I put the proverbial blinders on and only considered one outcome: the most desired outcome. As I knew all too well from my encounter with younger inmates jockeying for position, positive outcomes are not always possible; it's sometimes necessary to consider alternatives.

On-the-fly, reactionary thinking is what I learned in Juvie and on the streets. I acquired deep, analytical contemplation, in large part, from baseball. Mentors, like Rudy, helped me understand how the sport required planning and anticipation. Like life, situational moments require players to remain calm when presented with challenges. It's up to us as thinking beings to understand there are ramifications to the actions we take, both on and off the diamond. Like Juvie, baseball was teaching me how to better deal with the unexpected. It's this kind of critical thinking that makes me love baseball so much. So far, life had thrown me many curve balls, but at least I was beginning to grasp how to adjust to them.

Chapter Nineteen: Return to Insanity

I spent four months living at Rudy and Hanna's home. At the end of my stay, according to the State of Florida's requirements, I was "rehabilitated." I made another trip in a state-issued vehicle, and this time, I knew exactly where I was going. I returned home in November of 1982, and while I may have made some progress, my family had not.

It took two weeks for the violence and general dysfunction to escalate.

One afternoon, Eddie took it upon himself to discipline me. Up-close, I inhaled the smell of the ripped, stained sheets from my bed as he held me face-down, his elbows pinning me in place over his lap. He whacked me over and over with a wooden paddle. I fought to escape his grasp, but nothing worked. He kept raining down blows as I squirmed, trying to arch my back to get leverage on him.

During my struggle, I screamed and cursed until my mother walked into rescue me. "Help, mom!"

She stopped walking and merely looked at me for a good ten seconds.

"Do something. Please."

She walked towards us. *Thank goodness. I'm saved.* But as I continued to thrash for help, my mother clutched her fist and threw a right hook—not at my brother, but at me. That's right, my mother snapped, punching me in the face as hard as she could. Then she turned and walked out the door.

I was shocked, confused, and, quite frankly, pissed off. It was one of those moments in which everything paused. Time stood still. I stopped struggling. Not only were police officers, guards, and other inmates against me, *my own mother was too.* I had now been written off by everyone. My brother actually halted his onslaught because of his own disbelief. I quickly separated from him and took off running.

"What the fuck was that?" I screamed at my mother as I ran out the door. "You were supposed to help me! Fuck this house and this family."

That afternoon I walked around strip malls and neighborhoods, trying to keep myself busy. As the sun began to set, I worried about food and shelter. I needed money but didn't want to burglarize more homes or cars. I was trying to go straight so I wouldn't return to Juvie.

Eventually, I made my way to an open laundromat with no customers inside. This was the perfect place to hang while I contemplated my next move. I sat on a washer and swung my feet over the edge, pondering the different rooftops and alleyways I could sleep in. Realizing washing machines and dryers required quarters to operate, I wondered if I could find dropped change.

I hopped down and got on my hands and knees, looking on the floor and inside the machines. Then I crouched closer to the floor, recognizing most money would be *underneath* the machines. I laid there, wiping off pieces of lint sticking to my hair and cheeks, peering beneath the machine. I squinted, trying to find any thin piece of metal.

Jackpot! A quarter.

I reached out my finger, but it was too far back, and with a half-inch clearing, the distance was impossible. This was so frustrating. I looked around for something to help me pry the quarter from under the machine. After looking in the garbage can, I found my tool: a wire coat hanger.

I straightened the metal to give me distance while keeping the hook part intact. This allowed me to reach the wire hanger under the machines to dredge whatever was under there so I could easily retrieve it. After thirty minutes of maneuvering under each machine, I amassed five dollars in orphaned quarters. *Enough money for dinner.* I was proud of my perfectly executed—and legal—scheme.

After dinner at a fast food restaurant, I turned my attention to sleeping arrangements. It was going to be cold but sleeping indoors was not an option. During my wanderings, I came across an alcove-type area behind a convenience store. The small, fenced-in section housed some type of machinery producing heat. *Perfect.* Though clearly not a public area—the fence was locked and stood eight feet tall—I wasn't shaken by minor details. I needed a place to sleep and the locked fence could actually provide significant protection in the event someone (or something) happened upon me in the night. This was where I was going to crash tonight.

Because the adjacent convenience store was still open, and I had time to kill, I cased the area, gathering additional items for comfort. I picked up cardboard boxes to serve as my bed and additional shelter, placing them behind the building for later. Then I gathered larger sticks and rocks as well as a glass bottle. These items were necessary in the event I needed to protect myself against any raccoons, rats, or other rodents during the evening. Incidentally, they would also work well to protect me from other people.

As soon as the store closed, I scaled the fence and threw over my cardboard boxes, rocks, and sticks. I went up the fence and back down the other side with a glass bottle in hand. Setting up the cardboard boxes, I laid out my weapons within reach. Home for the night, I quickly fell asleep.

Chapter Twenty: Packing Heat

"What the hell are you doing here?!" I heard a loud voice say in a middle-eastern accent. Apparently, this convenience store owner had a habit of opening his business at the crack of dawn. He had also decided to check on the caged-in machinery I used as my personal heater.

"How did you get in there?" He stood outside the gate, fumbling with a large key chain, searching for the right one to unlock the fence.

"What?" I asked sleepily, clutching one of my large rocks. "I always sleep here."

"Bullshit. I am calling the cops on you, you little hoodlum."

Crap. That means back to Juvie.

"Hey man," I tried to negotiate. "I just needed a safe place to sleep last night. I didn't cause damage or anything."

"You're trespassing and I'm going to call the police." He continued to search for the correct key.

I had to react quickly. I was not going to allow him to call the cops. I sprang up, replacing the rock in my hand with the glass bottle. I started to scale the fence from the inside, straddling the top along the opposite side of the entry gate.

"What the hell are you doing? Get down from there now."

At last, he found the key and opened the lock.

"Don't come in here, man," I warned him, but he entered anyway. I raised the glass bottle menacingly. "I'm telling, you man. I will fuck you up."

He kept coming at me. "This is my property and I will go wherever the hell I want."

This guy was pissed at me, no doubt, but he made a crucial mistake. He entered the cage when I was at the top. I had my escape route.

"Okay motherfucker." I raised the bottle up further. "You asked for it."

I threw the bottle at his feet. It was never my intention to hit him. I just needed a quick diversion so I could jump down the other side and run. That's exactly what happened. The bottle shattered at his feet and he crumpled into a fetal position. Before he could realize he was unharmed, I hopped down, sprinting toward freedom.

"I'm gonna call the cops, you little hoodlum," he shouted after me, shaking his fist.

His yelling quieted as my pace quickened. I relied on the early morning glow from a few street lamps, dodging potholes and uneven pavement as my legs pumped wildly. The cold stung my eyes, but I kept them open, scanning for additional threats. I hoped the semi-darkness would help obscure my small frame as I disappeared into Hollywood's murky dawn.

I ran until I was out of breath, only slowing to a walking pace when I came upon the neighboring town of Davie. It was there I began looking for financial opportunities. As morning morphed to early afternoon, I realized I needed more money to buy food. I spent most of the day strolling around town doing whatever I wanted but knew I would soon need a place to sleep tonight. Obviously, my accommodations from the previous evening were not an option, and I didn't want to spend the evening in Davie since I wasn't familiar with the area. I began walking through various neighborhoods, back towards Hollywood. My goal was to avoid running into family or friends. I made up my mind I would revert to burglaries to secure cash for this latest venture. Convinced I would never go home again, I was willing to take chances to ensure I could survive on the streets.

Traversing a middle-class neighborhood, I debated my options. *A vehicle in the driveway? Not going there. Windows open with the sounds of a TV or radio emanating from inside? No shot.* I walked down more streets, passing house after house until I finally found the right one. Painted yellow with blue shutters and a small front porch, it looked devoid of activity. No cars were in the driveway. No neighbors were outside, milling about in their yards. Nobody appeared to be home.

I approached with the game plan I always used. I knocked on the door. No answer. I knocked again. No answer. I tapped the front windows. No response. No sound from a dog. *Things were looking good.* I made my way to the back and found what I was looking for: an entry point. The homeowners had left a window cracked open.

I removed the screen, then reached my hand in between the opened window and sill, carefully scanning the area. I wanted to make sure no neighbors saw me. Because the window was cracked just enough to get my arm inside, I could open it wider by cranking on the handle. In thirty seconds, I removed the screen, opened the window, and climbed inside.

My feet immediately met carpet. I looked around at the modest digs. A worn couch sat in front of a TV. The kitchen smelled slightly of cooked bacon and dish soap. Cleaned pots and pans for drying cluttered the sink. After inspecting the living room, I proceeded with my routine, checking all of the bedrooms and bathrooms to make sure there were no quiet occupants. Once I confirmed the house was clear, I searched for money, opening drawer after drawer until I found what I was looking for: an envelope containing $400 in cash. *Wow. This should keep me fed for a couple of weeks.*

I pocketed the cash, continuing to scour the master bedroom. After poring through every drawer, I turned my attention to the bedside nightstand. I found something there I thought could keep me safe. Usually I only looked for money, but this opportunity was too good to pass up. Plus, it would provide the ultimate protection. I pulled out a handgun.

I wasn't sure what kind of handgun it was, but it was mine. I held it in the air, pivoting so I could stand in front of a large mirror on the opposite wall. I pointed the gun straight at the mirror, holding it with both hands the way I had seen in movies.

"Make your move," I said. "Make your move and I'll blow your goddamn head off."

After a 10-second standoff with the man in the mirror, I decided it was time to go. Though I had never handled a gun before, I knew to engage the safety to avoid a misfire. I holstered it in my waistband and headed for the exit. Rather than escape via the entrance window, I closed it to a cracked position and left through the back door. I locked the bottom doorknob lock, then proceeded to put back the window screen. When I left, the whole place looked just the way I found it.

I walked around for another hour before finding my way to a fast food place to grab lunch. While eating, the gravity of the situation began to weigh on me. *I just stole a gun.* Before today, I had never even seen a gun up close, much less touched one. Now, I owned one. I felt empowered, but also anxious. I began to run through scenarios in my head as I picked at my burger and fries.

Did I really need a gun? Yes, especially if I ran into another psychotic child molester. But what if the gun accidentally went off and I shot an innocent person or, worse, myself? What if I pulled the gun out and the other person had a gun too? There was no way I could shoot first. Or, maybe I could.

I wavered between the need for power and protection, versus the fear of accidental misfiring. After lunch, I made my way to an open field, next to a large bank. I found a good-sized hole, probably dug by other kids. It was about six by five feet across and three feet deep. As an eleven-year-old, I couldn't resist. I jumped in. Folding my hands behind my head, I laid back against the inside wall of the hole, peering to the sky to consider my situation.

"What am I going to do with this damn gun?" I muttered to myself. "I want it, but I don't want it." I thought about throwing it away, giving it away, even selling it, but all of those scenarios were fraught with dangerous repercussions. Fifteen minutes into pondering, an idea hit me. *I could bury the gun. I already had a head start on the hole and could easily come back here if I ever needed it. Nobody would ever find it here—it was perfect.*

I lifted my head from the wall and began digging a hole into the side. I thought it best to tunnel into the sides rather than the middle. If the original diggers returned, they would probably dig deeper instead of wider. My wall assault resulted in a hole about a foot deep. As I reached for the gun, I realized I needed to put something around it as protection from the sand. I was no gun expert, but I was sure sand could ruin parts of it if it got inside. I kept the gun in my waistband as I hoisted myself out of the hole, searching the field for something to cover it. My litter-radar was strong and soon I found a brown paper bag.

Returning to the hole, I removed the gun from my waistband, double-checked the safety, then wrapped it in the brown bag. I shoved it into the hole, pointing the barrel end toward the ground. I figured if I ever came back for the gun, I wouldn't want it pointing up at me. After packing the dirt in as tightly as I could, I manipulated the ground, trying to make it look like the window I had just leaped through— exactly as I had found it.

Chapter Twenty-One: Seeking Shelter

Pinball was my thing. I could play it for hours, winning free game after free game. It was the only legal pursuit I consistently won, and it was three hours I could afford, financially and mentally. Whenever the novelty wore off, I would get food. On this particular night, I left the arcade to grab something at McDonald's. Heading towards the familiar golden arches, I noticed a germ-ridden playground. I had been on the streets for a couple of days now and I worried about the effects of my absence on my mother. Still, as I opened the door, breathing in the comforting smell of burgers and French fries, I knew I couldn't go home — I couldn't withstand my brothers' wrath again.

Later, as I crumpled the grease-stained bag, licking salt off my fingers, I thought about places to sleep. It was going to be cold again, so indoors was ideal but nearly impossible. I put my legs up on the booth seat across from me, peering around the restaurant. *Maybe there was a way I could get "accidentally locked in" here for the night. Perhaps I could hide in the bathroom during closing? Sneak in the utility closet while they locked up? Or I could crouch inside the garbage receptacle after they emptied it?*

Then it hit me. It was Sunday night. I could go to my elementary school. Given my skill at breaking into homes,

I could undoubtedly find my way into the building for the evening. Then I'd wake up early enough to grab my free breakfast before bolting for the day. It was the perfect plan. Until I got there. All of the doors and windows were sealed shut. There was no way in. I turned my attention to the portable buildings, which were smaller and stand-alone, designed to supplement the main campus.

I checked the portable doors. Locked. I considered the windows, but they were too high up for me. *Damn.* My plan was crumbling and the night was getting colder. After thirty minutes of searching for alcoves or other nooks to sleep, I began to lose hope. It was dark, and I was desperate. I slid my back down an exterior wall, wincing as I hit stone cold pavement. I stared at the ground, anxious thoughts swirling in my head as I crossed my arms across my body to stay warm.

Then I saw an opportunity. The portables were placed on top of block pillars, which held them two feet off the ground. Although I couldn't get into the portables, I could get *under* them. I walked over to the portables, bent down to get a view, then crawled beneath. Though I worried about critters and bugs that might also sleep there, the night's unrelenting chill drew me in.

Without a jacket, I needed to find a way to block the wind. It took a while, but I was able to dig a large enough hole for me to lay in, approximately four feet wide, four feet long, and a foot-and-a-half deep. I rolled into the cavity, crouching to keep warm.

Initially, the hole was perfect. It blocked the wind and kept me out of view. I wasn't sure if someone might look under the portable at night, but I recently had come to expect the unexpected so I prepared just in case. After a couple of hours, the temperature dropped. I don't know how cold it was on that November evening, but it was frigid enough for me to do something stupid.

Freezing, I pulled myself out of the hole and ran to the dumpsters. I found several large boxes, hauling them back to the portable, one-by-one. Some of them I used to cover the hole to block the wind. The others I ripped apart to create additional warmth.

During my travels earlier that day, I swung by the Ark, an old restaurant I frequented as a delinquent, often stealing money from the wishing well. Just inside the doorway, there were two things I always grabbed. The first were these chocolate-covered mints I absolutely loved. The other was a book of matches with the restaurant's logo, phone number, and address. The Ark's matches came in a small box and were made of wood, the type of high-end matches I always needed.

That night, I put the Ark's matches to good use (or so I thought). I pulled some of the cardboard boxes and paper products into the hole and set up a small compost. Then I lit the small fire and *voila*, I was much warmer. As the evening went on, I continued to feed it, dozing in and out, unable to fully fall asleep. After an hour or so, I grabbed a larger amount of cardboard, then placed it on top of the fire. I thought it would keep the blaze burning so I could sleep more than ten minutes.

I fell fast asleep, not realizing I left paper and cardboard just outside the hole, close to the fire. Within about fifteen minutes, I abruptly awoke to an intense conflagration.

"Holy shit!"

I sprang out of the hole, scrambling to kick sand up from the ground, trying with all my might to put the fire out. I pushed as much paper and cardboard as I could into the hole, then filled it with armfuls of sand.

The larger flames dissipated, but ashes smoldered inside the hole. Smoke enveloped the building, rising farther than I expected. I knew I had to get out of there before the fire department arrived—I sure as hell didn't want to add arson to my resume.

I scampered from underneath the portable, then took off into the neighborhood as the sun rose. Hearing sirens, I sprinted towards the McDonalds from the night before. I needed to put as much distance as possible between me and the school. Also, it was time for breakfast.

Chapter Twenty-Two: Unexpected Reprieve

It was now day three of this crazy excursion, and I already had two close calls. After running from the fire I started, I wandered neighborhood streets, fretting about the consequences, fearful the cops might pick me up at any minute for destroying the school. When they found me, I knew I wasn't going back to Juvie this time. Instead, they would lock me away in actual prison.

"*Kurky*," a voice yelled from a hundred yards away. "Kurky!"

I turned. "Shit," I said to myself. It was Tommy, charging after me on his bicycle.

"Kurky, you little prick. Where in the hell have you been?"

Instead of answering I took off running.

"Kurky, get your ass back here."

I knew I had no chance of escape with Tommy pedaling on his bike. He skidded to a halt in front of me, then grabbed me. "Listen, you little fucker. People are saying you burnt down the school."

My heart leaped into my throat. "I didn't do anything."

I struggled to get loose from him but he snatched me back anyway.

"Calm down, Kurky." Tommy tightened his bear-hug grip on me.

"Motherfucker. Get offa me."

"You need to go home. Mom is worried sick."

Mom worried? Really? That was new. It was my mother's right hook that sent me running off in the first place. That, of course, and the beatings from the person I was trapped by once again.

"Get on the handlebars and I'll tow you home."

Surprisingly, Tommy had calmed down, so I took him up on his offer, jumping onto his bike. I looked at the ground while he pedaled, relieved from running but completely freaked out about what I might have done. Tommy pedaled faster and faster, leaning forward to see in front of us.

"So. Did the school really burn down?" I asked innocently.

"I don't know. I saw a lot of fire trucks and shit over there when I went to look for you."

"But you didn't see any burnt buildings, right?"

"Not really. There were too many fire trucks and police cars to see."

"What made you think I did it?"

"I heard people say they saw a kid that looks like you running away from the school this morning. You better not have set that school on fire, you asshole."

I gripped the handles harder until my knuckles turned white. "How could I set the school on fire, Tommy? That's stupid. I would never do that."

We rode on for a minute or two before I started in with the questions again.

"Did anyone actually say I did it?"

"I don't fucking know," Tommy said, his irritation growing. "Did you?"

"No, no. Not at all," I paused. "But did you hear anyone say, 'Kurt did this or something?'"

The houses on our street passed by in a blur as we whizzed toward home.

"No, I didn't hear anything," he screamed over the wind in our ears. "They just said some blonde-haired kid was running so I assumed it was you."

"Well you shouldn't assume shit!"

"Fuck you. You don't tell me what to do. I'll throw you off this bike."

"Okay, fine," I slumped on the bar. "I just wanted to know if anyone said 'Kurt did this.' That's all."

Tommy slowed down to actually look me in the face. "Nobody said your name, so don't worry," he said, surprisingly gentle. "Now shut the fuck up."

I followed his instruction, not saying a word until we got home.

Chapter Twenty-Three: 'Til The Cows Come Home

The school never burned down. In fact, none of the buildings were damaged. Rumors ran quickly that morning, spurring my guilt and concern. Of course, I never wanted to damage the school. I just wanted to stay warm, so I was relieved to hear the school survived my dumb antics.

Unfortunately, I did not always learn from my failed plans nor past experiences. Though I didn't exactly have close pals, troubled youth begets troubled youth and my childhood years featured relationships with seedy characters. When I wasn't running around by myself, I hung out with individuals I loosely labeled friends. Of these so-called friends, three later committed suicide, two were incarcerated for much of their adult lives, and another was institutionalized. Not exactly the kind of pals your parents want you to bring home.

One of the aforementioned individuals, Jamie, was my partner for the crime that put me in my third stay at Juvie. My poor choices came to a head one dark evening in a neighborhood off Sterling Road. Prior to this, I had never burglarized homes or cars with an accomplice before, and that night I realized why.

Jamie and I cased the neighborhood around 8:00 p.m., looking for an opportunity to pick up money. Although I was more experienced with home burglary, Jamie insisted he enter the home while I stood outside on lookout duty. If anything looked suspicious, I was to alert him.

We seemed to find the perfect home. No cars in the driveway, no lights on in the house. No neighbors around. In fact, the adjacent homes were dark, too. It looked like nobody was home at either end of the street. As soon as we pushed the doorbell button, we heard a barking dog inside and Jamie immediately turned to run.

"Chill out man," I said. "You can't run off now. It'll look suspicious."

"What are we supposed to do?"

"Don't worry. I got this. Just get back over here."

"What do you mean, you 'got this'?"

"Trust me. It looks like nobody is home, so relax."

I rang the doorbell again, making the dog bark once more.

"Shit, man, let's just go," said Jamie.

"Just hold on a minute. I think we're good."

"We're not good. There's a fucking dog in there."

"A little dog. A very small dog who probably couldn't hurt a flea."

Jamie's beady eyes narrowed. "How do you know it's a small dog?"

"Listen to the bark. He's a little dog. Probably some type of poodle. Can't hurt you."

"You think so?"

"Definitely," I said, sensing my opportunity. "But if you're too scared to go inside, I will."

"No, no. I'm good. I can do this."

"Are you sure? I'm happy to go in if you'd rather stay as the lookout."

"I'm good," Jamie said like he was trying to convince himself. "But what if the dog comes after me?"

"Rub his belly."

Jamie's jaw tightened. "Seriously, man. What if the dog comes after me?" He paused, then answered his own question. "I'll just kill the fucking thing."

I wasn't expecting that. "*What?* No. You are not going to kill the little dog. That's fucked up."

Jamie was on a roll. "If he comes after me, I'm going to kick the fucker. If he dies, then he dies."

This didn't sit well with me at all. I balled my hands into fists within my pockets, watching uneasily as Jamie revved himself up to enter the house. I started to walk away, hoping he'd follow.

"You know what, Jamie? Let's just blow this place off. We can find another."

"No." Jamie remained still. "There's a lot of money here. I can feel it."

This was getting out of hand. "You have no idea what's in this house. Other than a dog."

Just then, the dog barked as if on cue. I wished I could pick Jamie up like the poodle inside and run. "Let's just go find another place."

Jamie acted like he hadn't heard a word I said. "No. You're right. He's just a small dog. I can handle him."

"*Jamie.*"

"I can do this. Stay on the lookout."

"Are you sure? It's no big deal to find another house—there's lots of good ones in this neighborhood."

"Nah. I'm gonna walk around the back. Keep a lookout, Kurt."

And with that, Jamie was off. I walked across the street, situating myself at the edge of a large cow pasture. In addition to having a great view of the street, I also had an escape route across an open field.

Jamie seemed to be taking his time inside the house as I continued to wait and watch. *What the hell is going on? I would've been in-and-out by now.* The clock was ticking. I knew with each passing second we were getting closer to getting caught. While acting as sentry, I made a significant mistake. I turned my attention from the house to the cows behind me in the pasture.

"Hey, cow," I whispered in my stupid, eleven-year-old foolishness. "What's up, fat cow?"

The cow continued to chew the cud in silence.

"Stupid cows," I muttered. Some of them stared back at me, their mouths moving in a circle. They found me uninteresting compared to their food.

As I was entertaining myself with the cows, our break-in circumstances changed. I finally turned around too late, only to see a car had pulled in the driveway. Its headlights were off and no one was inside.

Shit, shit, shit. I had to tell Jamie.

"Here, puppy. Here, puppy." I gave the verbal cue, yelling at the top of my lungs. "Come on boy, where are you?" I whistled, continuing to look for my "lost dog." Meanwhile, there was no movement within the house. I was getting nervous now. I thought about abandoning Jamie, but I couldn't leave him when he needed me most, even if our plan was nefarious. I continued to call for the lost dog, to no avail. Then, out of nowhere, a police car came bolting around the corner and into the driveway.

Fuck. This is not good.

Vroom! Another police car pulled into the front lawn. "Damn it, Jamie," I whispered to myself as my eyes darted in all directions. "Where are you?" My heart pounded in my chest as the second police officer stepped out of his car. When I tried calling again for my dog, it caught the attention of the officer instead.

"Hey you," the officer yelled. "What are you doing?"

"I'm looking for my dog. I can't find him anywhere."

"Come over here for a minute."

"What?" I replied as innocently as I could. "I'm just looking for my dog who ran away."

"Son, I'm not going to ask you again. Get over here now."

Time to run. I leaped over the fence, ran into the pasture, charging toward the other side.

"Stop right there!" the officer yelled, coming after me.

I hauled ass through the field, stepping in shit and dodging cows along the way. Incidentally, most of the cows took notice of me now. They seemed to be amused at what was transpiring—almost as if they were saying, 'Who is the stupid one now, boy!'

"Stop or I'll shoot!" The officer reached down for his gun.

I was halfway across the pasture. I wasn't sure if I heard him correctly so I kept running.

"I said 'Stop or I'll shoot'," he yelled again.

I definitely heard that order so I stopped, just feet from the other side.

"On the ground. *Now.*"

I knelt down in place, sweat dripping from my forehead.

"Hands on your head."

I did as I was told. Seconds later, I heard the jingle of steel handcuffs as metal clicked around my wrists. The officer escorted me back to the house, where a third police car had just arrived. They placed me in the back of the vehicle, immediately driving me to the police station for booking. I was back in Juvie.

Chapter Twenty-Four: Third Time's the Charm?

We pulled into the Juvenile Detention Center late in the evening and the place was dark. Most inmates were already asleep, and the tranquility of the halls put me on edge. I was used to the rowdy rough and tumble of boys. Instead, the eerie silence made Juvie seem even more threatening. I went through the usual process for check-in, which was just as humiliating and degrading as the previous two times. After issuance of standard clothing, bedding, and shoes, I was escorted to my cell.

I thought I was going back to Mod G-1 (the girls' Mod), but we immediately headed in the opposite direction. Anxiety filled me as we passed through the cold, dark corridors. I couldn't help thinking about what happened on my first trip to this rat hole. I had already vowed to myself I would not be a victim again. I would go down swinging if anyone approached me in that same manner. My mind raced as I planned how I might defend myself. I didn't know how I would do it, but no matter what, I was going to defend myself.

We continued on. Upon reaching the hallway fork, B-2 was on my right and B-1 was on my left. Just prior to the bend, I peered through the glass partitions in an effort to see Jerome. If my old friend was still here, at least I had someone to protect me—assuming, of course, he remembered me. Unfortunately, I couldn't see through the darkness. We continued on the left side of the fork. *Crap.* I was going back to Mod B-1. As I prepared to stop, the guard muttered something to me.

"Keep going. Straight up the hallway. This is where you'll be on this trip."

On this trip? What the hell did that mean? Surely, this was my final trip to Juvie. I was going to straighten my life out and say goodbye to crime forever. Later, I realized this was a sentiment many inmates bought into. It wasn't so easy to change. I entered Mod B-3 and the guards locked me in an empty cell. I made my bed, then sat on the edge, contemplating what would be in store for me next. I stayed up for a couple of hours, thinking things through as much as I could before finally falling asleep.

The next morning, I awoke at 7 am from the chaos of the Mod. My cell door opened. These were not metal bars like prison; instead they were solid wood with a small window about eight inches in width running along the right side. The window was incredibly thick to be as shatterproof as possible. I had personal experience with the window's strength because I tried (unsuccessfully) to break it on more than one occasion.

As we lined up for breakfast, I immediately took inventory of the other inmates. This Mod seemed different. There were quite a few younger kids (eleven to twelve years), as well as some children with physical limitations. The latter didn't necessarily have physical disabilities, but deficiencies, like being small for their age. AKA: easy targets. I later discovered they had been victims, and this Mod served as a protection.

After breakfast, I hung around the Mod for a while, taking inventory of my surroundings. I watched some television, engaged in small talk, and acclimated to my new home. Just as I was settling in, the guards opened the front door and in walked someone I thought I wouldn't see again—Jamie.

At first, I wasn't sure what to do. I was pissed we got caught and I blamed it on Jamie's insistence he be the one to break into the home. To make matters worse, we were now facing a charge of armed burglary because unbeknownst to me, Jamie decided to bring a hunting knife with him. While I was mad at Jamie, the reality was I could have decided *not* to break into the home or *not* to run around on the streets that evening. I could have accepted responsibility and accountability. I could have— and should have—made better choices, but those options never entered my mind.

Once I was done wondering whether or not I wanted Jamie in the same Mod with me, I realized his presence could actually be an advantage. We could watch each other's back. In this place, it was imperative to find people to trust. In that regard, having a friend from the outside was a plus. Jamie and I stuck together for the most part, but his peculiarities soon became disturbing. One night, I walked into Jamie's cell and found him sorting small pieces of glass on his window sill. He stood next to his bed, picking up each piece with one finger, balancing them with the concentration of a competitive poker player.

"What's up with all the glass?" I asked.

Picking up a piece on his fingertip, he reached it out to me, smiling. "Oh, I have plans for these."

"What kind of plans?"

Jamie turned toward the window sill. "They're my way out of here."

I waited for him to explain, but he returned to examining the glass as if it was his own evil science experiment. There was a long pause. Twenty seconds turned into what seemed like five minutes. I grew agitated. "What the hell is your plan, Jamie? You're not making any sense."

"You see," Jamie replied as if he was in another world. "I take these shards of glass and I eat them. Then I take some more and stick them in my eye."

"Are you fucking kidding me? That's the dumbest shit I've ever heard. You're going to kill yourself."

"No, no, no." Jamie raised his hand. His eyes shifted to the door, then he walked over and poked his head outside, making sure a guard wasn't nearby. I stayed near the window, watching his every movement. Jamie came back to me, whispering. "I'm just going to hurt myself a little. If I eat this glass and put some in my eye, they'll have to take me to the hospital. They can't treat me here."

I threw my hands up. "What happens if it damages you to the point of no return? What happens if you go blin—"

"Nothing's going to happen. I'm not worried about it."

"Well, I think it's very stupid, but do whatever you want." I turned and walked out, shaking my head in disbelief.

Later that afternoon, Jamie put his plan into motion. I didn't see him swallow the glass or insert the pieces into his eyes, but I did see the horrible results. I was playing cards with some inmates when two guards sprinted into Jamie's cell. When they came out, Jamie was holding onto his eye, blood streaming down. He screamed in pain as he exited the Mod. Jamie's plan worked. He was taken by ambulance and never returned to Juvie, at least not while I was still incarcerated. I would never see Jamie again as things were about to change for me in a way I didn't see coming.

Chapter Twenty-Five: Rise of Baby Gator

News and rumors of Jamie's stunt made their way around the institution. One group of kids claimed Jamie was beaten up and forced to eat glass. Another blamed the guards. Other rumormongers blamed what happened on a failed suicide attempt. Though I knew the truth, I ignored the gossip and went about my business. Just in case Jamie tried to make up another story, I didn't want to blow it for him.

A few days after Jamie's grand exit, I was playing *Spades* with some other inmates when they called my name over the loudspeaker.

"Kurt Varricchio, please report to the guard's station immediately."

"Oh, shit, Baby Gator. That's you," chided one of the inmates, snatching his set for winning the round.

"Baby Gator" had become my new nickname in this Mod. According to others, the moniker came from the combo of my young age and violent temperament when pushed too far. Over the years, I'd learned to strike first whenever fighting because I usually battled older, bigger kids. If they got in the first punch, I may not have a chance to retaliate. Usually, if I swung first, I swung often—there was no middle ground. I didn't always win, but at least I got in my shots, making a good showing. After a couple of fights on this contentious Juvie stay, the nickname stuck.

Another inmate whistled at the loudspeaker summons. "Shit, Baby Gator, you goin' down now."

I threw down my cards. "Shut up, you guys."

Sauntering to the guard's station, I tried to hide my apprehension. I worried they might ask me about Jamie's incident. Worse, they might even blame me for it. During the twenty-yard walk, I ran worst-case scenarios through my head. It didn't help my anxiety.

"I'm here," I told the guards as confidently as I could.

"You have a court appearance today."

My breathing returned to normal. "Okay. When do we leave?"

"Now."

Twenty minutes later, I sat in a courtroom chugging out justice like a well-oiled machine. Defendants and their attorneys (most often, public defenders) rolled through an assembly line of hearings, legal fates sealed by swift adjudication. Typically, it went like this: counsel would make a request, then the parties would discuss the matter for 30 seconds. Afterward, the judge would lay down his order. Bespectacled, with deep frown lines, he ran through cases like water, trying to keep pace with an overburdened system.

I was the last defendant to be called. "The State of Florida versus Kurt Varricchio will now be heard in Judge's chambers," the clerk announced.

I may have been confused by these words, but the no-nonsense bailiff wasn't. He steered me to an office located behind the bench. Here, several people sat around a large conference table, including the judge's clerk, a couple social workers, my public defender, the prosecutor, some so-called experts, and finally, to my pleasant surprise, my mother.

I gave her a small wave. "Hey, Ma."

"Hi, baby."

Her smile stopped at her eyes. I could tell she was taking mental inventory of my physical wellbeing. The meeting didn't begin well. They wouldn't let me sit next to her. Instead I was sandwiched between my public defender and the gruff bailiff.

"Why can't I sit next to my mom?"

Nobody said a word so I asked again, this time louder.

"For security purposes." The bailiff didn't look up from his pad of paper.

"Defendants aren't allowed physical interaction with family."

"Well, that's bullshit."

I yanked the chair out from the table, slamming it on the floor. A loud thud echoed across the chamber. The social worker sighed. My defender acted like he didn't notice. When the judge walked in, I grabbed the chair back and sat down, scowling.

"Good morning." He took his seat at the head of the table. "Let's begin. We have with us Kurt Var-ri-chi-cho for armed burglary—"

"It's Va-Ricky-O." I sat up straighter. "VA-RICKY-O! It's not that hard."

The judge didn't appreciate my interruption but was surprisingly understanding. "Okay, then. I'm sorry about that. Va-Ricky-O."

I grinned at my mother for my small victory.

"Do we have a recommendation from social workers on this case?"

The two social workers looked at each other. Then the one with the sallow face and tight hair bun stood up. "Yes. We advise the son be removed from his home. Permanently, your Honor."

What? Her words felt like a punch to the face.

"And what is this recommendation based on?"

"Your Honor, there is absolutely no home supervision. The children are permitted to do whatever they want, whenever they want. The mother has no control. Garbage litters the property and the home is infested with roaches, insects, and other vermin. Numerous animals live at the home that appear to be uncared for."

As the social worker delivered her scathing report I ground my teeth so hard one of the experts turned to me. I gave him the death stare. *Fuck these Suits. This shit might be true, but no one gets to say it to my mother.*

The social worker with the bad complexion droned on. "In summary, Ms. Varricchio is unfit to care for her children. In addition to the defendant, the mother has three older boys and a younger daughter who lack basic needs. Ms. Varricchio lacks the requisite parenting skills."

Barely able to sit still, I was becoming visibly agitated by the second. My blood boiled.

"Also, your Honor, Ms. Varricchio's young daughter is only three-and-a-half and runs all over the neighborhood whenever she wants. The mother simply lacks control and—"

"Why don't you just shut the fuck up?" I jumped out of my chair.

The bailiff threw me back down. Holding back tears, I continued to yell. "You have no idea what you're talking about."

My public defender tried to calm me down. I grew hysterical as I was again forced into my seat. My mother stared at me, her eyes watering.

"Son, you will sit in that chair and remain quiet," the judge ordered.

"No, this is all complete bullshit! You don't know what it's like to be us. None of you do."

The judge had had it. "*Kurt.* You WILL remain in your seat and not interrupt these proceedings anymore. Do I make myself clear?"

I refused to answer so my public defender answered for me. "Yes, your Honor." His hand remained on my shoulder. "He understands."

In seconds, the judge accepted the social worker's recommendation to permanently remove me from my home. At the proceedings' conclusion, they escorted me from the chambers. Right before I left, I turned to see my mom one last time before leaving in the Juvie van. Tears ran down her face. As a parent now, I can only imagine how she felt in that moment.

Chapter Twenty-Six: Baby Gator Snaps

"There he is. Baby Gator in da house!"

"Did you enjoy your trip, motherfucker?"

On edge from my trip to court, I ignored my "friends." For the first time ever at Juvie, I didn't give a shit about showing emotions. I sat slumped against a wall in the back of the Mod with my head in my hands.

"Damn, man, what happened?" a twelve-year-old with the thin beginnings of a mustache asked.

"Nothing," I lied. "Nothing at all."

"Man, it don't sound like that," another inmate with homemade tats on his back and neck said. "They fuck you up, nigga?"

I was getting increasingly sick of this interrogation. "No, man. I just want to chill for a bit."

The others got the message and left me alone. I played with a piece of orange lint on the floor, wondering what it meant to be "taken away" from my mother. I had already been to a group home and it wasn't so bad. If that was my only option, then I would be able to get by, hopefully surviving the next few years until I turned eighteen. The other possibility was one that scared the hell out of me: Lake Okeechobee Juvenile Detention Center.

Affectionately known as "Chobee", this ghastly detention hall was designed for long-term stays. Known far and wide as the toughest facility in Florida, repeat offenders were often sent here when all other options failed. Representing the worst of the worst, we all heard horror stories of a huge pool at this facility where kids mysteriously drowned. All kinds of frightening lore about Chobee echoed throughout other Florida institutions. The unofficial motto was to the point: "Chobee bound. If you can't swim, you're bound to drown." The possibility of being sent to Chobee chilled me. Kids at Chobee were often jumped by gangs or sexually molested. If I ended up in Chobee, my life was over as I knew it.

The longer I sat there worrying, the more it enticed other inmates to mess with me. I had ignored something fundamental. Kids in Juvie prey upon weakness. It all went back to mastering the pecking order.

"Yo, Kurt," one of them said. "You missing your mommy?"

Refusing to take the bait, I stared at the floor. The guy with the half-moustache approached with a swagger. "Hey man, motherfucker asked you a question. You better answer it."

Eye contact was a good precursor to confrontation. I didn't want to give the authorities more reason to send me to Chobee so I stayed aloof, pretending to study cracks in the floor like they were architectural wonders.

"Hey, punk," yelled a third kid. "You better answer our question."

"I'm not in the mood to answer your questions. I want to be left alone."

I might as well have put a big sign on my head reading, "Beat me." Like chum to a shark, inmates encircled me, sadistic gleams in their eyes.

"Oh, little gator baby wants to be left alone," said the original bully to the others, making them laugh. I finally looked up to see the group. Four of them stared down at me. I was not in a good position to defend myself. Beyond being outnumbered, I was also sitting on the floor against the wall, so they had leverage.

Recalling Rudy's tactics about minimizing risk, I formulated my options. Two kids stood at my right, another two on my left. In the middle, a clear path led to the guard station. I might be able to get there but I needed a diversion. I couldn't wait for them to start attacking. I had to act. I placed both of my hands against the wall behind me, finger tips pointing to the ground with my arms bent to provide me a catapult off the wall. Then I used an audible distraction.

"What did you say, guard?" I yelled.

The idiots took the bait. As soon as they turned, I launched myself through the gap and into the Mod's center. I was still outnumbered, but at least I was off the floor and away from the wall. If they were going to jump me, they would have to do it while I was standing.

"Get over here, you little fucker," the biggest kid demanded.

"Nah, I'm good."

"We're going to fuck you up, you little asshole," said the gang's leader. He advanced toward me, pressing me up against the station's window.

I tapped the glass. "Guards. These guys are messing with me but I'm trying not to fight."

The two guards smirked at each other. One pretended to write a report while the other stirred his coffee. "Figure it out," he said, sipping from his mug.

Figure it out? What the hell was there to figure out?

"There is no figuring it out! There's four of them and one of me."

The one writing the report checked his watch, put his feet up on the desk, and pretended to snore, making the other guy laugh.

"Please. I don't want to get into trouble by fighting."

The snoozing guard pretended to fall out of his chair which only made the other one laugh even harder.

"Are you just gonna sit there while these guys mess with me?"

"Not unless you have some creamer out there," the one with the mug joked.

Once again, those who were supposed to help me turned their backs on me. *Weren't they hired to protect kids like me?*

"Get me out of here now. I need to go before I do something stupid."

More jokes and laughs from the guard station. By now, the group of four had picked up on the guards' indifference and closed in.

"Looks like they want a show," said the leader, approaching closer.

"Get me the fuck out of here. NOW!"

I head-butted the glass window as hard as I could. Though I saw stars, I was wired from the fear. I punched the window as hard as I could with each fist before turning my aggression to the stalking group of four. They were still in disbelief over my head-butting, so I caught them by surprise. My knuckles rammed into their skulls as I landed punch after punch.

"You should've gotten me out of here earlier!" I yelled. I continued to throw haymakers until the guards grabbed me from behind. Kicking and screaming, I laid into them too. "I told you motherfuckers to get me out of here! I fucking told you!"

The guards threw me into an isolation cell as I continued to hurl insults. Giving the door a final kick before walking away, they left me alone and broken. My knees buckled and I collapsed in a ball. I was alone in my cell, symbolic of the fact that I was now also alone in my life.

Chapter Twenty-Seven: A New Turf

Night after night in my isolation cell, I visualized Chobee. I imagined myself walking into the facilities: the inevitable cat calls, the gangs of four and five, the sadistic head nods intimating violence to come. Images of hands flashed through my mind. Hands grabbing me, punching me. I pictured the pool's edge. Falling in. Drowning. As I looked up through the murky water I saw sneering faces—

"Varricchio!" a guard called. "Get your stuff together. It's time."

I blinked up at the cell door. "Time for what? Am I going back to the Mod?"

"Not today. You're getting out of here."

Did he mean they were sending me to the C-word?

The guard stretched the door open further, nodding towards my meager stack of belongings. "Get your stuff."

I liked the fact I was getting out of here, but I worried where I was going. It took me thirty seconds to pack up the few items I owned. Afterwards, we made an immediate right out of isolation, heading down the long hallway to Receiving, where they gave me the clothes I came in with.

"Go in there." The guard pointed to a small room. "When you're done, bring back your standard issues and we'll check 'em off for you."

After changing, they whisked me into a van.

"Where are we going?" I asked.

"Oh, we got a long ride ahead of us today," said the middle-aged driver with thick, hairy arms and a beer belly.

My heart sank. Chobee was "a long ride" from Fort Lauderdale— approximately two-and-a-half hours away. To get my mind off Chobee, I thought of my mother. Though her infrequent visits were short and Marie-focused, at least she came. *What if they put me someplace hours away?*

I remained silent as we motored along the interstate. At last, my anxiety got the better of me. "So, exactly how long of a ride do we have ahead of us?"

"Oh, about five hours—at least. Yeah, we gonna be driving a while."

"We ain't going to Chobee, are we?"

The driver turned halfway around. "Chobee? You wanna go to Chobee?"

"Hell no! I just want to know where I'm going, that's all."

"Oh. Okay. Well we ain't going to Chobee, so don't worry."

This was the best news I'd heard in a long time. I wanted to hug that redneck driver.

"We're heading toward Tampa, son."

I'd never been there before. "Why Tampa?"

"No idea. All I know is I'm supposed to drop you off at some social worker's office over there."

This meant I was going into a group or foster home. No more institutions. A chance to go to a real school with real kids. Although I was being displaced, things were looking better. My anxiety subsided as I began to take in sights across Alligator Alley, including a few eagles soaring high in the sky and alligators sunbathing on the canal banks. I searched for any baby gators but didn't find any.

Continuing on, I plastered my face across the window, absorbing every bit of the sawgrass-lined canals. Five hours later, we reached Tampa where I transferred to another car driven by another social worker. At least I got to sit in the front seat this time.

"Right in front of you is the Bucs stadium." He pointed out the window.

"The Bucs?"

"Yeah. Tampa Bay Buccaneers—the NFL team."

I stared in amazement at the immense facility, imagining what it must feel like to see a game live. "Man, I don't know what I'd do if I ever went to an NFL game."

As soon as the words were out, I regretted them. The chances of going to an NFL game were slim to none. Habitual juvenile delinquents like me didn't partake in such activities, especially *poor* habitual juvenile delinquents. My amazement dissolved to disappointment as I sunk deeper into my seat. After another thirty minutes, we pulled into the neighborhood. As usual, I became hyperaware of my surroundings. Street after street left me confused and apprehensive. I went on high alert. Something was very wrong.

Chapter Twenty-Eight: A New Beat

The social worker knocked on the door three times, then gave me a slight smile that did little to ease my tension. *Didn't he know we were both the odd ones out here?* I peered over my shoulder once more, then jumped as the door opened. There stood my new group home family. My new African-American group home family.

"Hello, Mr. and Mrs. Butler. I have with me Kurt Varchi-rio," the social worker stumbled.

"It's Var—" I started to say. "Ah, forget it."

Growing up, I never had racist thoughts, and of course, don't have them now. Still, my experience with black people in Juvie shaped my younger self. Countless times, I saw fights in which black kids beat up loners. It was always three or four black kids jumping a single kid (white, black, Hispanic, it didn't matter). The assault by the group of five during my first stint was like that and the experience stuck with me. Similar to how a black person might feel strange around whites after being abused by some of them, I now felt nervous to be around black people I didn't know. Therefore, when I first arrived, I was really nervous—not so much because of the Butlers—but because all of the other kids in this neighborhood were black.

"Hello, Kurt," said Mrs. Butler.

Arthritic and slightly overweight, Mrs. Butler was a stay-at-home-mom who ruled her house. She cooked, she cleaned, she laid down the law.

"Get your stuff and come in," she told me. "Greg will show you to your room."

Mr. and Mrs. Butler were in their early fifties, hardened by a lifetime of long working hours. They feared God, attended church, and kept their house spic and span. Although the Butler's owned a washing machine, they didn't have a dryer so every afternoon, Mrs. Butler could be seen in the front yard hanging clothes to dry on the clothes line. The key was to get them down before the rains came late in the afternoon, a job she delegated to us kids.

Their son, Greg, was about my age. Upon meeting that afternoon, we both gave each other a once over. I wasn't sure we would click. Other than the fact he was black and I was white, there were other underlying issues. To begin with, I was coming into his home, infringing on his turf. Greg was used to having unfettered access to his home, including his bedroom, which he now had to share with me. Not only that, he was accustomed to getting all of the attention from his parents. A new kid like me threatened the balance.

In spite of a rocky first meeting, Greg and I managed to generally get along. He taught me several things, not the least of which was how to dance. As I said, the Butlers were a religious family and we would go to church every Sunday. Their place of worship featured an all-black congregation passionate about showing their love for Christ. They had a full band: electric guitars, drums, multiple keyboards, several other instruments—as well as a choir with belting, powerful voices that could be heard up and down the streets. They jammed like no other when it came to singing the gospel.

Children of the church were also expected to be vocal about their praise of God. Every Sunday, all the kids gathered in the center aisle before marching up to the choir stage. The band would play as the kids swayed in unison singing the lyrics, *"Jesus makes a way out of no way."*

The first time I tried the march to the front, I stood out for more reasons than one. First, I was the only white person in the entire church. Second, and most embarrassingly, I had no rhythm whatsoever. I zigged when everyone else zagged. I couldn't hold a tune and flailed like a fish out of water. There was no doubt who the new kid was, but I sucked it up and proceeded to the front like I was told, accepting the fact I must look like a complete idiot. Eventually, during all of the holy fanfare and gospel boogying, I made it to my spot, taking my place amongst rows of singing children. No matter how hard I tried, though, my rhythm was off. Kids went to the left and I went right. They clapped on the rhythm and I missed the beat.

It was embarrassing, but I participated anyway because it was expected. I could see the congregation watching me. In spite of my earlier misgivings about being here, lots of folks offered well-meaning smiles my way. I honestly felt they were excited to see me try. I will always remember how gracious these individuals were. They weren't making fun of me. They genuinely loved seeing the little white boy trying to fit in and I fed off their enthusiasm.

After services, I walked out with the Butlers, Greg beside me. I couldn't help noticing even when my group-home brother walked, he seemed to be stepping to a beat. Meanwhile, I trudged along, flatfooted as ever.

"Sorry, I messed up my part of the service," I said to everyone, slipping into the Butlers' vehicle. "I'm going to work on it. I promise."

Mr. Butler looked back with a shake of his head as he reversed. He had salt and pepper hair and soft brown eyes. "God don't care how well you do, so long as you are there to praise Him."

"That's the truth," Mrs. Butler added, nodding.

I nodded back. I'm sure they were right but I still felt embarrassed. I turned to Greg beside me. "You mind working with me on that marching stuff?"

"Yeah. Let's do it when we get home."

Later, I leaned against the bedpost as Greg showed me the first step. He had taken off his dress shoes and slid around in his white, calf-length socks.

He led the march and we circled the bedroom like wannabe soldiers. Occasionally he would abruptly stop, then remind me to always watch the kid in front for pacing. When I tried to follow his example, he pulled my arms down and told me to relax. "Let the rhythm move your body."

I marched in place, my arms hanging like unstable, refrigerated gelatin. "I don't think it likes my body."

"Well, it would if you relaxed."

Next, we pretended to be on stage. "You gotta hear the clap from the music. Do you know who does the clapping?"

"Uh, us?"

"No, the drummer. Now relax and feel the music."

I attempted to do what he said for the next three hours. Two of those were spent just on my march, which may or may not have fully improved.

In spite of my clumsiness, Greg was patient. Somehow, I think helping me helped him. His instruction allowed a white boy to 'get it', a serious accomplishment within itself.

The following week, I put my new moves to the test. It was show time. Greg's refrain to "relax" reverberated in my head as I marched in unison with the others. As the music swelled, I clapped, sang, and swayed from side-to-side, not like my previously awkward self, but now in sync with the rhythm. When I gave up overthinking it, heeding Greg's words to let the music guide me, I fell in with everyone, soaking up the collective flow. I stopped worrying and let it happen. I was loving life.

This experience taught me the value of commitment—not just from my own actions, striving to become a better participant in church—but also from Greg's selfless dedication to help me. When one commits to a worthy objective, working diligently to achieve it, seemingly impossible obstacles disappear. Peering out into the congregation, I could see the looks of stupefaction on churchgoers' faces.

"Whoa," said an older lady in the front aisle, looking right at me. "Little white boy brought it."

Turning to look at Mr. and Mrs. Butler, I saw them smiling their approval. I felt like a star and I owed it all to Greg, who, in spite of our differences, found it in his heart to help me.

Chapter Twenty-Nine: Second Class Citizen

Although Greg and I made peace with each other working on the church march, our differences remained the same and, with those differences, came conflict. Greg and I would argue over anything. Sometimes these arguments escalated into pushing and shoving matches, but never a full-blown fight because either Mr. or Mrs. Butler were there to intervene. Until Leon came.

Leon was another child for whom Mr. and Mrs. Butler agreed to provide a home, and he was also African-American. Unfortunately, Leon was a constant reminder that no matter how hard I tried to blend in or how many times I clapped to the beat in church, I was still the white outsider.

On the day of his arrival, Leon, Greg, and I stood in the bedroom we were now to share. The two beds Greg and I had been sleeping in sat perfectly aligned across from each other. Meanwhile, a third bed had just been added to the top of Greg's bed to form a bunkbed. Since I had been here longer than Leon it seemed reasonable for me to keep my bed and to have Leon use the top bunk.

Leon didn't see it that way. "I want it."

"It's mine already. No dice."

"That's not fair." Leon turned to Greg. "Why should he get it?"

Before Greg could answer, I cut in. "'Cause I've been here longer."

"So?"

"So, I get it."

"Screw that."

Greg stepped in. "I'll be the referee, you guys." He put his hands behind his back. "Tell you what we'll do. I'll pick a number between one and ten. Each of you can guess it and the closest one to the number gets the bed."

"No way," I said. "I've got dibs already."

But Greg wouldn't budge on refereeing. Something smelt rotten about this whole thing but I had no other choice. I was outnumbered.

"Fine. Six." I peeked over at Leon to make sure he wasn't looking behind Greg's back.

"Three," said Leon.

Greg showed us his hands. He held three fingers up. Somehow, Leon magically guessed the right number. "Leon's right! It was three. Sorry, Kurt. Guess you gotta re-make your bed up top."

I was upset as I sensed injustice once again. Later, when I approached Mrs. Butler about Greg's tendency to play favorites with Leon, whether it be what show we watched, or where we sat at dinner, she said what she always did: "Stop bugging me with your nonsense."

Soon, everyday became the Greg & Leon show. The final straw involved something petty: a game of hide-and-seek in the yard. It all started innocently enough. I searched while Greg and Leon hid. I found Greg easily, then it was my turn to hide.

We played several rounds this way. Every time I hid, either Greg or Leon always found me, yet neither of them ever found each other. This began to seem odd to me, especially given the fact I usually had a better hiding place than either of them.

Finally, after six or seven rounds, I realized Greg and Leon were collaborating to find me. When I peered around a corner, I saw Greg speaking with Leon. Leon then pointed in my direction, scampering behind a car.

"Found you, Kurt," Greg triumphantly exclaimed.

"That's bullshit. You guys are cheating."

"What? We ain't cheating. How are you gonna cheat at hide-and-seek?"

"I saw you and Leon talking and he pointed over towards me. That's cheating."

As Greg and I argued, Leon made his way over.

"What's up Kurt?" Leon asked. "You're it."

"No way. You guys are cheating. You're it, Leon."

Both of them stood their ground in unison against me, declaring me to be it.

"Screw this! I quit."

"Fine," Greg said. "Be a quitter. Baby."

I started to walk away.

"Yeah, he's a quitter," Leon chimed in as Greg joined him. It was bad enough dealing with one of them, but I had two kids making fun of me.

"Shut the hell up, punks."

"Come here and make me shut up," Greg demanded.

I smelled a trap. "You know I can't come after you because your mommy and daddy will blame me for starting it."

As I turned to walk away again, I felt a tug on my shirt. "Do something," Greg demanded.

I pushed Greg away. "Don't touch me."

Greg gave me a push and the game was on. Our hands became weapons as we wrestled to the ground. I got in some good punches and kicks, but Leon had to ruin it.

"Mrs. Butler! Mrs. Butler!" he yelled.

Instead of Mrs. Butler, Mr. Butler came flying. He did not look happy. He went straight for me, throwing me off his son. I started to say something in protest, but Mr. Butler cut me off.

"I don't want to hear it! You knock this foolishness off, Kurt."

I looked to Leon and Greg. Both of them were silently laughing at me behind their hands. In a split second, I knew who would always be punished for every fight. I knew who would always be blamed for everything bad that happened. I flashed to an earlier memory of my own mother walking past my brother to punch me in the face. I did what I always did when people unfairly mistreated me. I ran.

I didn't know the area, but I knew I had to get out of there. I darted out of the neighborhood and kept going. I had no destination, but my legs kept moving. I only stopped when I couldn't catch my breath. By now, I was miles from the Butler's home. Several hours passed. Though I needed money for food, the fear of Chobee staved off my burglary inclinations. Instead, I scoured dumpsters for bottles to return. Finding nothing, I moved onto option two: loitering.

This convenience store appeared to be part of a family-owned gas station and looked like it may have friendly customers. Although I wanted to ask them for money, I realized people didn't like to give to beggars—even kids—so I decided to provide something of value to "my customers."

As people walked in and out of the front doors, I served as their doorman. I would open the door to folks entering the store, greeting them with a "good afternoon" or "hello", then politely close the door behind them. Returning to the front door from their shopping, I would greet them again, then ask for change. It actually worked! I was almost to my five-dollar goal when the store manager came outside. A burly man with a grey button-up shirt and a thinning beard, he grabbed the door handle from me.

"You need to get out of here."

"Why should I leave? I'm not interfering with anything."

"You're disturbing my customers. And loitering. Leave or I'll call the cops." He tried to shut the door on me, but I put my foot out to stop it.

"Call the cops? Are you serious? I'm not doing anything bad."

He turned and went back inside. I thought I might have gotten him to see the error in his judgment, until a police car pulled up minutes later. I still didn't think I was doing anything wrong, so I figured negotiating would be better than fleeing. The ruddy-faced officer with a buzz cut and double chin stepped out of his squad car. "What are you doing here?" he asked.

"I'm trying to make money being a doorman. It's either this or steal it, which I don't want to do."

He stood by the trash can, putting his hands on his protruding belt buckle. "You need to leave, kid."

"Why? You can't tell me to leave. I'm not doing anything wrong."

"What's your name?"

"Kurt. And that's with a 'K,' not a 'C.'"

"Kurt what?"

"Kurt Varricchio. And that's with two r's and two c's."

The officer's hands went from his belt to his radio. He turned his head, mumbled something into it, then looked back at me, his posture straightening. I inched back, wondering what he was going to do.

"Kurt, come with me." He grabbed my arm, pulling me towards his car.

"Let go of me."

He grabbed me tighter. "Are you the runaway from that group home in Plant City?"

"What runaway? I have no idea what you're talking about. I don't even know what a runaway is."

"You know exactly what a runaway is. You're coming with me."

He pushed me into the back of his car. At the time, I thought this treatment was very unfair. After all, I was just helping people as an unsolicited doorman. I didn't realize running away from a group home was a serious offense, but it was serious enough to land me another stint in Juvie, this time in Hillsborough County. More and more I felt injustices stacking up against me. No place was safe or permanent, not my home with my mother, not Juvie, and definitely not these group homes.

***

I kept my guard up during this short Juvie stay. Unfortunately, though, some kids saw me as an easy target because of my age and size so I was constantly being bullied by older, bigger kids. Because of my insurmountable fear of going to Chobee, I kept my emotions in check and simply rolled with the punches. That is, until, one day, when I reached my limit.

Growing up in South Florida, I loved the Miami Dolphins. That year, the Dolphins had a stout defense, known as the "Killer Bees." The Dolphins were led by A.J.

Duhe, Bob Baumhower, and the brother defensive back tandem of Lyle and Glenn Blackwood. The "Killer Bees" defense ranked first in fewest total yards allowed and carried the Dolphins to Super Bowl XVII. Incidentally, that same Super Bowl would take place during this particular Juvie stay.

I recall getting up that Super Bowl Sunday and looking forward to watching my beloved Dolphins take on the Washington Redskins and their juggernaut offense led by Running-back, John Riggins, and Quarterback, Joe Theismann. The game wouldn't start until 6:00 p.m. so I had a lot of time to kill. Since it was important to me to be front-and-center for the Super Bowl, I set up my viewing position around 3:00 p.m. that afternoon, watching all of the pre-game shows leading up to kickoff.

Alas, kickoff came and there I was: right upfront rooting for the Dolphins. Halfway through the first quarter, David Woodley hit Jimmy Cefalo on a 76-yard touchdown reception and the Dolphins were on top, 7-0. The teams battled back-and-forth and the "Killer Bees" held their own against the high-powered Redskins' offense. Excitement from the game thrilled me so much that for the last hour and a half, I even forgot where I was and what was waiting for me on the backend of this stay in Juvie. Nothing else seemed to matter. *My team was close to winning the Super Bowl.*

At the half, the Dolphins were leading 17-10. Nature called around this time so I got up to go to the restroom. Every kid in Juvie knew how important this game was to me as I wore my emotions on my sleeve. Most of them were supportive of the Dolphins as well, so it made for a fun evening...so far.

When I got up to leave, I specifically claimed dibs to my seat, making sure the others knew I would be right back. One of the unwritten rules in Juvie is that you keep your seat in front of the television if you have to use the bathroom. Although we didn't have a lot of respect for much of anything, we all respected this unwritten rule. One kid, however, either didn't get the memo or didn't care, because he was sitting in my chair upon my return.

This punk was a bigger guy who enjoyed picking on us younger boys. Although I had ignored him on numerous occasions, I had no choice but to address him now. If I didn't defend my position, other inmates would notice, and life would become even more difficult for me in this place.

"You're in my seat," I told him, standing between him and the television. "I don't see your name on it," he smugly replied.

The fact he took my seat pissed me off enough, but his flippancy pissed me off even more. "Dude, everyone knows I was sitting there."

"Sorry, DUDE," he replied arrogantly. "You leave, you lose your seat."

Of course, he knew this wasn't the rule, but he insisted on being a jerk. I tried to keep my cool even though I was fuming and all eyes in the Mod were on me. I had to take a stand to show I would not be victimized by these bigger kids.

"So," I asked, my fists clinching. "Are you going to get up or not?"

"Think not." He smirked. As he turned with a shit-eating grin, seeking the approval of the others, my time arrived. Balling up my right fist, I threw everything I had into a hook across his jaw. I knocked him clean out of that chair, then dove in for more, landing haymakers, one after the other, and screaming expletives with each punch.

I had hit my max with this stuff. Not only did this kid disrespect me in front of every single inmate in my Mod, he took away the little happiness I had: watching my team in the Super Bowl.

The guards rushed in and pulled me off of him, but not before I landed a significant amount of shots. I established my street cred by taking on a bully and beating him at his own game. As the guards escorted me to a separate cell, many of the younger kids came up to me, offering congratulatory pats on the back, while some of the bigger kids nodded to me.

Unfortunately, lost in all of my newfound glory was the crappy fact I had to watch the rest of the Super Bowl peering out the tiny window of my cell door.

***

Not long after this incident, I was told I would be leaving Juvie. As the Mod doors opened, the guard called my name. "Get your stuff together," he said. "You're going back home."

"Back home? To Hollywood?"

"To where?"

"My home...in Hollywood."

"Oh, no no no. I thought you were from Plant City— that's where you're going. Back to the same place."

Back there? That's not my home. Now, I was totally disappointed. It turned out I was going back to the Butler group home. *How could I function there? How could I get along with Greg and Leon who totally excluded me from everything?*

Although I wasn't excited about returning to the group home from where I just ran away, it certainly beat staying in Juvie. I decided to suck it up, focusing on how I would explain to Mr. and Mrs. Butler why I tried to escape. I wasn't looking forward to that conversation, but I knew it was coming and began running scenarios through my head as I stared out the window on the drive back.

Mrs. Butler took my arrival in stride.

"Hello Kurt," she said as I exited the car. "Your room is in the same spot as it was last time."

"Thanks." I sheepishly grabbed my small bag of belongings to trek into her home. Mrs. Butler stayed outside to speak with the social worker, joined moments later by Mr. Butler.

I never did provide an explanation to either of them because, quite frankly, I couldn't muster up the courage. Either way, I think they forgave me and, for that, I vowed to be a better kid. Things went well for a few weeks as I tried hard to make the right decisions and say the right things.

As most things went in my life during these formative years, however, my second stay with the Butlers eventually turned south. Greg and Leon continued to pit themselves against me for everything. It was frustrating and, as was often the case, when I grew frustrated, trouble wasn't far behind.

One day, our playing outside led to a minor dispute. In an effort to take the high road, I walked inside the house to explain the problem to Mrs. Butler, but she didn't want to hear it. "Go figure it out and get out of this kitchen," she said.

As I was walking out the front door to the yard, Greg was walking in. Since we were both stubborn, neither of us ceded way to the other. Battle lines were drawn.

"Out of my way," Greg demanded.

"No. You get out of mine."

As Greg tried to bull his way through the front door, I stood my ground and we jostled. He pushed and I pushed back. Then he threw a kick with his right leg, which I caught and grabbed with my left hand. I had him! As I held his leg in my left hand, I clinched my right fist, ready to deliver a right hook. Just as I wound up, Mrs. Butler came running. "Don't you dare hit my boy, Kurt, you let him go right now!"

I flung Greg's leg while simultaneously pushing him. He landed on his back in the front yard. I looked to Mrs. Butler, then to Greg, then to Leon nearby. Then I took off down the street. I was gone once again.

***

After a long run, I slowed to a walk for several hours through various neighborhoods and communities, making my way east. My goal was to walk all the way back to Hollywood. During this journey, I kept a keen eye out for police cars because I didn't want to get caught like I did last time. Every so often, I would see several of them along the road and, each time I did, I would do whatever I could to avoid being detected.

Several hours later, I began to get hungry. I needed a way to get money to buy food so I began to panhandle at a convenience store. I didn't receive a single cent. After thirty minutes of trying, I gave up, continuing my walk east.

I proceeded for another hour or so as the sun disappeared behind me in the west. Things became more challenging as the temperature dropped. I grew more tired, hungrier and colder. Approaching another convenience store, I walked inside to warm up. I also asked some of the patrons for spare change. My requests were not well-received by the store manager and he asked me to leave so I did.

I continued walking but found it increasingly difficult with each step. I was at the end of my rope and realized, begrudgingly, I had to make a tough decision. I needed food, clothing, and shelter. I vowed not to commit any more crimes because I knew I was already on thin ice and didn't want to be sent to Chobee.

After another hour or so of walking, I spotted a phone booth. It was time for me to make another tough decision. I entered it and quickly closed the door, hoping being inside would keep me warm. Although it cut down the wind, it wasn't any warmer than outside. I sat there contemplating whether or not I wanted to take this next step. At last, I picked up the phone.

"911. What's your emergency?"

"Hi, uh... I'm calling about some kid that may have been reported missing," I stuttered, shaking.

"What kid?"

"The one who ran away from that group home in Plant City."

I coiled up inside the booth, squeezing into the corner to stay warm, trembling from cold and fear.

"Okay. What can you tell me about him?"

"Well...I'm him."

I continued speaking with the operator, describing my frustrations. This particular person seemed compassionate enough, so I confided in her as she kept me on the phone. We talked until a police car pulled up.

"He's here," I informed the operator. "I'm gonna go now."

"Okay, Kurt. Thank you for calling. That took courage."

I hung up and walked out to the police officer. He opened the back door and I jumped inside. I knew where I was going, but I also knew it was warm, it provided three meals a day, and offered a place to sleep. At the moment, a fifth trip to Juvie seemed like an exceptional offer.

Chapter Thirty: Hard Labor

After the Butler debacle the system spat me out again. The next car ride was similar to the last, with me sinking further and further into my seat as the newest social worker attempted small talk.

"So where are you fr—"

I cut her off. "Where am I going this time?"

This lady was short with dark hair and glasses. She kept her eyes on the road as she spoke. "You're going to a group home. You're going to live with the Mitchells."

"That's great. What color are they?"

"Color?"

"Yeah. What color are they? Black? White? Brown? What color?"

She finally took her eyes off the road to glance at me. "I'm not sure, Kurt. Why does it matter?"

"Why does it matter? Why do you think it matters? I'm white. The last time I was in a black home it didn't go so well because I didn't fit in."

"I'm sure you'll be fine with whatever color they are."

Whether or not she was right was beside the point. At eleven-years-old, I couldn't comprehend how to handle tensions I felt were attributable to race. Although Mr. and Mrs. Butler were exceptionally kind people, I felt as if I was on the outside looking in at their home and I wasn't mature enough to handle it. After turning down a dirt road similar to Rudy and Hanna's, we arrived at the Mitchells' home.

Like that family, the Mitchell's were hard-working, blue-collar, country folks. Mr. Mitchell was an ironworker for the local union who put in long hours to make ends meet. He believed in giving his employer an honest day's work for an honest day's pay and he was highly regarded in the industry. Similar to Mrs. Butler, Mrs. Mitchell was a stay-at-home mom who kept after the kids. They had a son and a daughter—both older who no longer lived at home. They occasionally made cameo appearances to the group home kids, but otherwise their house was filled with non-biological children.

The Mitchells' brand of discipline was one I had never experienced. Rather than whips or belts or smacks, they chose hard labor as punishment. Naturally, I experienced their chosen discipline on several occasions, but there were two instances that stood out above all others. I don't recall why I was mad one day, but I told Mrs. Mitchell she could go to a place people don't like to be told to go.

She paused, then went in the garage to grab something. She returned with a machete. "Take this, Kurt. Go out back and start chopping down some of those trees."

Seriously? Chop down trees? I almost laughed aloud as I walked away. Since the Mitchells were country folks, they lived on a fairly large piece of land. In the backyard, rows of trees ran parallel to each other in an open field, backing up a couple hundred yards.

"Stupid punishment," I mumbled under my breath as I started whacking at a tree base. Within fifteen minutes, my first tree fell—a small one with a six to seven-inch diameter.

"Timber!" I yelled, thinking I would stick that to Mrs. Mitchell.

I walked into the house. "Done," I declared confidently. "Here's your dumb machete back."

"Uh-uh. You're not done until I say you're done." She put it back in my hand, steering me to the door. "Now get back out there and get to work."

"What? Are you kidding?"

"Nope. Go. And don't you leave that area until I tell you to."

"Fine," I screamed as the door shut behind me. "This is such bullshit."

"You just earned more time for that, Kurt. If I were you, I'd stay quiet."

I channeled my anger into more tree-whacking. The second one, though bigger, came down faster than the first.

"This is bullshit," I seethed. "Absolute horseshit."

As the second tree collapsed, I yelled toward the house. "Here goes number two, Mrs. Mitchell." Then, I gave the tree a final kick so it would be a clean break. "Hope you're fucking happy."

After that, I continued to whack tree after tree, cursing this brand of punishment. By my fifth, the whacking had taken its toll. My arms limped to my sides after each swing and sweat dripped from my face. Raw from gripping the machete, the skin on my hands blistered, ripped, and bled, slowing my pace. Mrs. Mitchell's punishment was actually working. *She was winning.* Several hours later, I was too tired to be upset. My body ached and my stomach rumbled. Weakened, my aching arms swung blindly as I struggled on.

"How are you feeling?" I heard Mrs. Mitchell come up behind me.

"Fine." I could no longer put up a fight. "Just doing what you told me to do."

"I see," Mrs. Mitchell smiled. "You've done a good job. You can stop now. I think you learned your lesson."

"I don't want to have to do this sh— I mean, stuff anymore, so I guess so."

I finished cutting down my last tree, then stumbled back to the house. All told, I was out cutting trees with that machete for the vast majority of the day—seven hours. Unfortunately, I was a slow learner back then....

The second instance of Mrs. Mitchell's unconventional discipline involved another form of manual labor: shoveling. Since the Mitchells lived off the beaten path in a small, wooded neighborhood, they sometimes did things differently, including disposing of certain types of waste. They would actually burn trash in a large hole in their back yard. After getting into trouble another day, Mrs. Mitchell proposed another one of her quirky discipline ideas.

"Kurt," she said sternly. "Come with me."

She led me to the back of the lot, fifty yards away from the house. "See this garbage hole? I'm gonna need you to expand it. Grab that shovel and start digging. Consider it discipline for what you did today."

Again? More manual labor?

"Fine," I said. I dug, and dug, and dug. Hour after hour, I did it, cursing my existence. At one point, I stood in the center of a hole measuring 12 feet across, 12 feet long, and 4 feet deep. Mrs. Mitchell would later tell me all she could see was the shovel periodically popping up out from the hole as I unloaded shovel after shovel of dirt.

"Okay, Kurt," I finally heard from beyond the mound. "You're done now. If we have any more issues, you can come back out here and dig some more. Maybe all the way to China."

She chuckled at this last line, but I didn't find it quite so humorous.

After that I tried to keep my nose clean. For the next few months, I (nearly) became a model citizen at the Mitchells' house. Later, I realized how effective these people were in disciplining without ever laying a hand on me. This was significantly different from what I had experienced in the past, and, as I would soon discover, the Mitchell's shared values with another couple I was about to meet—a couple that would change my life forever.

Chapter Thirty-One: Game-Changer

"Kurt," Mrs. Mitchell called from the kitchen. "Can you come here?"

I backed away from the TV, my eyes still glued to the baseball game until the last second when I almost collided with Mrs. Mitchell.

"I have someone you need to speak with." She smiled, handing me her phone.

"Hello?" I said into the receiver, as Mrs. Mitchell exited the kitchen.

"Well, hello, Kurt," an upbeat female voice said. "My name is Sandy. You'll be coming to live with me."

"Hi, Sandy," I replied nervously. "Are you my next group home?"

"My husband and I are actually foster parents and we're looking forward to welcoming you to our home. We are very excited."

A foster home! The prospect seemed so much better than a group home. In my mind, a foster home meant permanence. No more going from group home to group home with periodic stays in Juvie. I immediately bombarded Sandy with questions. We talked for several minutes. I learned she and her husband Joe had a pool in their backyard and nearby relatives, and that I would be able to walk to my new middle school. Sandy managed a travel agency and Joe was a high school teacher. They didn't have any children of their own, but they did have a beautiful black Labrador named Annie. I loved dogs and, of course, I loved swimming, so everything sounded great.

Within a matter of days, I was on a flight to Fort Lauderdale. It was the first time I had ever flown and it was a rough journey. The flight from Tampa to Ft. Lauderdale was a short one so we used a smaller aircraft. Unfortunately, we flew through a thunderstorm, experiencing turbulence. Although I never thought we were going down, I did get knocked around good enough to use the barf bag conveniently located in the back-seat pocket. The people sitting beside me weren't thrilled, but I was too distracted by thoughts of my new foster home and Annie to care.

Once I landed in Fort Lauderdale, I was met by a social worker named Barbara Greenbaum at the airport. I had met a lot of social workers in my short life but Barbara was the real deal. Years later, she would tell my future wife that when she received my case file, she was shocked. In her entire career, she had "never received a child with a rap sheet like [mine]." It was so lengthy she wasn't sure anyone would want to take me. Yet somehow, she managed to convince Sandy and Joe to take a chance and I am forever grateful for her persistence.

Barbara and I pulled into the driveway of Sandy and Joe Evancho's home on June 9, 1983. Sandy and Joe lived in a middle-class neighborhood on a corner lot. My new parents were already waiting outside for me by the front door. They seemed genuinely excited to meet me, which already made me feel better about the transition. As I stepped out of the car, Sandy quickly made her way to me, wrapping me in a huge hug. She was nearly six feet, and I felt overpowered by her long arms and tight squeeze.

"Hi Kurt. We are so happy to meet you!"

My natural family wasn't exactly the warm, touchy-feely type so I didn't know how to respond. "Uh, hi." I reciprocated with a small hug. "Nice to meet you too."

Sandy let go and motioned toward Joe, who gave me a slightly embarrassed wave as if apologizing for Sandy's affection.

"Hi Kurt." He extended his hand.

I sighed with relief. At least I knew how to shake a hand. "Hi, Joe. Nice to meet you."

That first day couldn't have been more different than any other of my life. Sandy was so kind and welcoming. In fact, she was more like a kid in a candy store, beaming from ear to ear as she looked down at me in my Sunday best. I wore white MacGreggor sneakers (the pride of K-mart at the time), blue jeans and a blue/red Hawaiian shirt. I figured I wouldn't get another opportunity to impress them so I tried to put my best foot forward. Later, I learned Sandy was a huge fan of Hawaiian culture; she even danced with a Polynesian group, so the Hawaiian shirt was definitely a hit.

Joe also seemed excited to meet me, but I could sense his reservations. Although he was one of the best men I ever knew, and I became fortunate enough to call him "father", Joe wasn't good at masking his emotions. I could certainly understand why Joe would have concerns about me coming to their home. As my mile-long rap sheet attested, I didn't have the best reputation.

For a long time, Sandy and Joe hoped to adopt a small child or infant. They had been waiting for two years without success. When they received a phone call about an at-risk youth in need of a more permanent foster home, I didn't exactly check off any of their boxes. I don't think my type was high on their wish list. In fact, I'm willing to bet my type wasn't on their list at all. Despite this, the Evancho's took me into their home with open arms.

After saying goodbye to Barbara, Sandy instructed me to drop my stuff off in my new bedroom. I had a room all to myself! Then, they took me to the pool area where Sandy had set up a buffet for lunch. Over ham and cheese sandwiches beside their adorable dog, Annie, Sandy explained she was from Maine and that her entire family still lived there with the exception of her sister, Sis. Sis lived in Pembroke Pines about twenty minutes away. The normalcy of having an aunt and cousins felt unreal to me. Later, we would end up doing most everything with Sis and her family.

Joe's family, at the time, lived primarily in the Cleveland and the Chicago areas. Although Joe's mother passed away, he was close with his father, who would drive down to Fort Lauderdale every winter to live with them. Over the years, I grew close to Grandpa Evancho because he was always home when I returned from school.

From the get-go, Sandy and Joe treated me just like one of their own. They took an active interest in my well-being and wanted to make sure I was given a fair opportunity. They were especially concerned with me getting a fair shot in school. Sandy even went to war over me with Plantation Middle School.

When I first moved in with Sandy and Joe, I had just finished my 6th grade year at a middle school in Plant City. Similar to most other schools I attended, I was labeled "emotionally disturbed" (ED) and was subsequently placed in remedial classes. Apparently, the powers-that-be felt my emotional baggage might be distracting to 'normal' students so I was placed in the same classes as other apparently disturbed children.

Though I was used to these kinds of things, Sandy was livid. When the administration insisted they knew what was best for me, Sandy quickly convinced them otherwise.

Upon Sandy's advocating, I was mainstreamed with 'regular' students for the first time in my life. Although I didn't know it at the time, this was critical because I was able to witness another new normal. These kids had many similar challenges to us 'ED' kids, yet they dealt with them differently. They weren't ready to fight at the drop of a hat, and they certainly didn't curse their teachers. They struggled academically, just like we 'special' kids did; they also had the same concerns regarding social issues, bodily changes, and anxiety. Despite what the officials would have had Sandy believe, I actually had a great deal in common with these regular kids.

That first year at my new middle school was challenging. I wasn't used to attending class every day and I certainly wasn't accustomed to doing regular homework, studying for tests, or working on school projects and papers. Sandy and Joe continued to encourage me, though, stressing the importance of education, especially when it came to reading and expanding my vocabulary. No one had ever done anything like this for me before and the results were tremendous.

Previously, the only stuff I was ever good at were bad things, like crime. School became a way for me to be recognized for something positive, like grades. This might seem simple, but for me, it was an integral part of my physical, mental, and emotional journey outside of Juvie. Sandy was also very patient with me, encouraging me at the same time. For instance, if I did well on an exam, she would say, "Wow, you got an A on that test! That's wonderful. I know you studied really hard for it. Now, imagine what you could do with all of your classes if you did the same thing." She would also recognize me for other accomplishments, even if they were insignificant to others. She knew how important praise was to me—how it could propel me to bigger and better achievements.

Although improving in many ways, my violent and turbulent past still provided major obstacles. In my early days with Sandy and Joe, my tongue was razor sharp and my temper volatile. After all, my Juvie nickname was "Baby Gator." I was not accustomed to what most people would call 'normal living.' Perhaps it was a product of sleeping on top of laundromats or in isolation cells, but every night I slept in the fetal position, often wetting the bed.

In all honesty, I was severely emotionally damaged when I moved in with Sandy and Joe. Too often this emotional damage manifested itself in my actions, both voluntary and involuntary. I was clumsy. It seemed I spilled milk at dinner on a weekly basis. I couldn't say why. Perhaps it had to do with the fact I wasn't used to eating dinner with family at a table. One night, I happened to spill the milk again as usual. For whatever reason, this time I didn't feel like cleaning it up when Joe told me to. I had no reason to disobey him—after all, I was sitting at his table beside his wife, eating their food, when I bumped my glass, soaking Sandy's meatloaf and half the table.

When I refused to do as Joe said, Sandy stepped in. "Kurt, would you please grab some paper towels? The milk's dripping onto the floor, honey."

I could have easily done what Sandy asked. After all, she was being so nice about it, and the paper towels were less than five feet away on the counter. The problem was I didn't like people telling me what to do and I especially didn't like the way Joe was glowering at me, so I told her no.

"Tell Joe to get the fucking towels."

While Joe was usually a mild-mannered man, he could be set off with the right words or actions. He slammed his fist on the table, making the plates jump. Milk cascaded down the table, pooling onto the floor.

Sandy stood up. "I'll just get the towels."

Joe stopped her. "No. You sit. Kurt, would you please hand me the towels?"

Sandy turned her sweet look on me, but I ignored it. Instead, I glared back at Joe and shook my head.

Joe's eyes flashed with rage. "KURT."

"Honey," said Sandy. "Just let it—"

"No, dear. He needs to learn respect." Joe leveled me with his eyes. "I'm not asking this time. Get. The. Towels."

Drip. Drip. Went the milk down the table. Joe waited for me to do what he told me.

"No way."

"Do it, Kurt."

"Fuck off. Get 'em yourself."

Before Joe could get up, I did, throwing my chair across the living room. Sandy gasped. Joe managed to dodge the chair but it crashed into the sofa and wall, taking down a lamp.

"Oh my God!"

Furious, Joe came rushing after me.

Chapter Thirty-Two: Differences

Joe chased me into my room in back of the house. I heard Sandy's footsteps thudding across the tiled floor as she raced to keep up with us.

"Joe, it's okay. Just calm down. He didn't mean anything!"

Entering my room at top speed, I rushed to slam the door shut but Joe caught it early. Using his foot to wedge the door open further, he pushed back from his side. I jostled my end, desperately trying to close the door on him.

"Just stop it, Kurt."

"Leave me alone. Get away."

Joe was bigger than me by about six or seven inches and much stronger. He quickly shoved me backward. I fell onto my bed, screaming curses at him, thrashing to get free. Above me I could see Sandy's face stretched in fear. "It's okay, Kurt. It's okay," she said.

I lashed out at Joe, kicking and punching. I was like a rabid dog. One of my punches landed on the side of his face. Enraged, he snatched both my arms, pinning my hands down by my head. I had never seen him so mad.

"What is your problem?" he yelled. "Don't you know we love you?"

"No!"

Sandy put her hand to her mouth like I had just kicked her. "No?"

Hot tears rolled down my cheeks. "I know you don't. If you did, you'd hit me."

Joe stopped dead in his tracks. Stunned, he dropped my arms and stood back.

Sandy bawled, collapsing on the bed beside me. "Oh, honey."

Even Joe began crying. He wrapped me in his arms alongside Sandy. "We love you so much, son."

They dried my tears and we calmed down. Then, the three of us had a long talk that lasted throughout the evening. Joe and Sandy told me what they just heard was like a light going on. They had no idea just how deeply rooted my problems were. This experience, though difficult and highly emotional, was a seminal part of my development as well as a pivotal learning opportunity for Sandy and Joe. They realized I associated love with violence because that's how I grew up. My brothers would say they loved me while beating me or soon after.

"I'm only doing this, Kurky, because I love you," Tommy would say.

It sounded reasonable to me at the time, but obviously it wasn't. Though I grew much closer to my foster parents that night, especially Joe, I continued to act out in socially unacceptable ways. I carried myself around my new school like I did in juvenile hall: with a chip on my shoulder. Naturally this created strife amongst my schoolmates, leading to numerous disciplinary problems.

Sandy fielded most of the school phone calls. Almost weekly, she got one from the principal detailing my indiscretions and issues. Poor Sandy. She was already managing a large company. I can't imagine the added stress those stern phone calls had on her. Nonetheless, whenever needed, she would trek down to the middle school for the obligatory parent-principal meeting.

By the time I was placed with Sandy and Joe as a foster child, I was considered a "runner." Whenever things got tough— whether through my fault or someone else's—I took to the streets. It was my modus operandi for dealing with conflict and problems. Until now, this was how I handled adversity. Even after Sandy and Joe told me they loved me, I continued to run. If they tried to discipline me, I ran. If I didn't want to do what they told me to do, I ran. If I was bored, I ran.

One day, my new parents asked me to help them clean the house. As one can imagine, kids don't like to do chores. This was especially true for someone like me who never had a clean house growing up. The way I saw it, having to clean up would take me away from a number of other fun things I would rather do. Therefore, accomplishing this task was not priority one on my list.

However, Sandy and Joe were insistent I did what they said.

"Kurt, we would like you to cut the grass, clean the garage and clean your room today," Sandy cordially requested.

"You want me to do what? That seems like a lot of work for a Saturday."

"Yes, dear. We all chip in so we can get it done faster and everyone can enjoy the day."

"Well, how about you two do it and I'll enjoy my Saturday," I replied in my customary smart-ass manner.

Both the content and the delivery style of this last statement didn't sit well with Joe and he let me know it. "Now, Kurt, you need to watch your mouth and not talk back to Sandy."

In retrospect, this was a reasonable request from someone who welcomed me into their home. But I was thick-headed and short-tempered. "Well, I'm not your slave, so I don't think I'll be doing any work today."

I could almost see Joe's blood pressure rising. "You will not talk to us that way. You are living in this house and you will help keep it clean."

"Fuck that."

"*Kurt.*" Sandy looked like I just slapped her across the face.

Before Joe could say another word, I blew up. "I'm fucking out of here then."

With that, I ran out the front door. Joe and Sandy gave chase.

"Kurt, get back here now," Joe demanded, his voice reaching an elevated level. Despite their pleas for me to stay, I took off down 70th Avenue, made a left on Sunrise Boulevard, and headed into another neighborhood. I may have had no idea where I was going, but it didn't matter. Eventually, I reached the Mercedes Movie Theater where I caught an early evening showing of *Risky Business*. Not a bad way to kill time, I thought. *This will teach Sandy and Joe to question me. Who the hell do they think they are, trying to get me to clean their house? This will show them who's boss.*

While my young mind was consumed with trying to ascertain why Tom Cruise was dancing in nothing but a button-down Oxford and his underwear, I tried to distance myself from my interaction with my new parents. By the time the movie ended, my mind was at ease. I had made my point to Sandy and Joe. *I* was the one in charge—not them—I'm sure they got the message.

Though wanting to impress my point further by staying out later, the reality was I spent what little money I had on the movie ticket and it was way past dinner time. I was hungry, and stealing money from a car, house, or any other person or place was not an option. Accordingly, I made my way back to Sandy and Joe's house.

My reception at home was mixed. Sandy was thankful I made it back safe, but Joe was mad I left in the first place. Certainly, both emotions were warranted given the circumstances. After calmly discussing what happened I retreated to my room for the rest of the weekend. Unlike my former home, there were non-physical, yet strong punitive measures in place here. Sandy and Joe grounded me.

Another running away incident became one of those formative life moments. I cannot recall what prompted me to run on this occasion, but I do remember the reunion with Sandy and Joe that followed. Upon returning, Sandy told me in no uncertain terms she had reached the end of her rope with my running antics. Though she normally greeted me with a big hug and some tears whenever I came back, this time she appeared more resolved and cold.

"Kurt," Sandy said sternly. "I'm glad you're home safe and sound, but we need to have a discussion regarding your running habits."

"Okay," I said smugly. "What do you want to discuss?"

"This needs to stop. Now."

While I agreed with her, I wouldn't admit it.

"Each time you run away from us, it hurts us," Sandy explained. "It takes an emotional toll and I can't deal with this anymore."

I remained nonchalant. "Okay."

Sandy took a deep breath. "You need to decide right now if you are going to continue to run or if you want to stay with us. There are no bars on the windows and no locks on the doors that you can't open. You are free to come and go as you want, but the running away cannot happen again."

I was put off by Sandy's assertiveness, but I continued to listen.

"I love you. Joe loves you. We consider you our son."

I said nothing, careful not to reveal the slightest bit of emotion.

"But if you want to leave, then leave for good, but know this: you will not be coming back. You will not take any of the things we bought you: clothes, games, toys or anything. You will only take what you came here with. That's it."

Pinned to the corner, I continued to grow more irritated, but didn't say a word. Sandy's delivery was different this time. I sensed she wasn't bluffing.

"Now you go back to your room and when you've made your decision, you come out and let us know."

I did as I was told, slamming the door behind me as I flopped onto my bed. *How dare she make demands of me? Who in the hell does she think she is? I should just pack my stuff and go.*

While these were my initial thoughts, products of my bruised ego, I understood living at Sandy and Joe's was probably the best scenario for me. Though I was a gambler growing up, I was a calculating gambler, and not stupid. After contemplating Sandy's offer, I returned to the living room to confront her. While I was gone, Joe had entered the room.

"I'll stay," I told them both matter-of-factly.

"Okay."

Sandy and Joe gave me a hug and I never ran away again.

In my adult years, I learned Sandy was seriously concerned I wouldn't accept her ultimatum due to my chronic stubbornness. She told me how she shed multiple tears over this potential scenario while she and Joe awaited my decision. I applaud her—and thank her—for taking a stand, demanding I make such a decision. It was time to dispense with running away from my problems. While the initial demand was meant to address a major problem for me at that time, the life lesson I learned remains with me to this day.

From that moment forward, I learned to face my challenges and obstacles head-on rather than turning (or running) away from them. Finding resolution is so much more productive than running from reality.

Chapter Thirty-Three: A New Varricchio

After numerous behavioral incidents during my 7th grade year, things started to improve. Gaps began to spread between the principal's phone calls, and I started performing better in school. Eventually, I promised Sandy and Joe I would try to stay out of trouble at school altogether, and I did, except for one small business opportunity.

When I was in 8th grade, *Now and Later* candies were a big item. Kids loved the chewy, flavorful taffy squares, though we weren't allowed to have candy in school. One day, I was eating a banana-flavored *Now and Later* (my favorite) when another kid approached, asking if I had more to share. I told him I did but if he wanted any, he would have to pay me for it: a nickel per piece.

"Okay. Here's a dime," he said. "I'll take two."

I took the money, gave him his candy, and walked away. The thing is, in the '80s *Now and Laters* came in small, six-piece packs. Back then, they cost ten cents per pack. My first customer paid me ten cents for two pieces, meaning he paid for the entire pack and only took 1/3 of them (two out of six). I enjoyed the other four pieces for free. Suddenly, a business venture was born!

That afternoon, I walked to a convenience store after school with a dollar in my pocket. "I'll take ten packs of

Now and Laters," I said proudly. I slid a dollar across the counter as if making a million-dollar investment.

The clerk picked my dollar up. "That'll actually be $1.05."

"What? They're 10 cents each."

The clerk chuckled. "You forgot about sales tax."

"Fine. Give me nine then." I returned one of the packs to the shelf, paid my $0.95 and went on my way.

The next day, I made sure people saw me enjoying my *Now and Later* candies at school. My previous customer walked up to me, his mouth watering.

"Do you have any more *Now and Laters*?"

"Why, yes I do. I have a couple different flavors. You interested?"

"Do you have green apple?"

I reached into my duffle bag. "Twenty-five cents gets you the whole pack. And that's a better deal than yesterday because you're getting six instead of five, so it's like getting one free."

"Okay," the kid said. "I'll take it."

I handed him the pack of candy in exchange for the quarter. He started to walk away. "Hold on." I grabbed him by the shoulder. "If you know of anyone else looking for candy, send them my way."

That afternoon, I unloaded eight of the nine packs for twenty-five cents each. My earnings on those eight packs, represented a profit margin of 250%. I started calculating numbers. If I purchased twenty packs at ten cents each, that would cost $2.10 (including tax). I could then sell those twenty packs at $0.25 each, generating $5.00 in sales, thereby claiming a profit of $2.90. This is exactly what I did the following day.

As word spread, my profits soared. I had an entire duffle bag dedicated to my candy operation. Unfortunately, the administrators caught on. Kids were eating *Now and Laters* all day, every day. When a few got busted for eating candy in class, they ratted me out. As I walked into the principal's office, the interrogation began.

"Kurt," the principal said, "We received feedback from your classmates saying you've been selling candy at school. Is this true?"

I had to think quickly and come up with an idea—a kind-of white lie. "Oh no. I don't believe I sold anything to my classmates."

"Are you sure about that?"

"Yeah, I'm sure. Not a single classmate."

The principal looked miffed this interview was taking longer than he'd intended. He didn't know I had been through several interrogations with police investigators, so I was a little more polished than other kids.

"Well, Kurt, I have students that specifically told me you sold them candy. What do you say to that?"

"Who told you I sold them candy?"

"That doesn't matter. What matters is you have been identified as selling candy at school, which is against school policy."

I saw my opening and the antecedent for an eventual career in semantic legal maneuvering. I would play on the "classmate" comment. To me, a classmate was someone in the same class as me. I took six classes; how could I know *which specific class* he was grouping me into in terms of 'classmates'?

The principal sighed. "Kurt, let's quit playing games. You're selling candy to your classmates and that's against school policy."

"So, I don't get to challenge what these other 'classmates' said about me? That doesn't seem like a fair shake to me, Mr. B."

The principal reached for his phone. "Let's just call your mother and deal with it that way."

After speaking with Sandy, I agreed to cease operations. In the following weeks, my candy business dissolved, momentarily. I eventually re-opened it, but ran it underground, imploring kids not to disclose their source. I told them if I was busted again, the operation would cease forever, and they would not be able to get any more candy at school.

Eventually, teachers began to notice an increase of chewing in their classrooms, but none of the kids told on me. Despite this, Sandy got a call about me distributing candy again. I vehemently denied wrongdoing, but Joe outsmarted me by searching my room. Despite my best efforts to conceal the evidence, he found my duffle bag. Though my operation was dead, I learned much about running a business, no doubt, paving the way for future, legitimate endeavors.

***

Things had vastly improved on the home front. I was getting good grades, no longer running away, and establishing firm ties to my school and community. Eventually, I became so integrated into Sandy and Joe's family they considered adopting me. I turned them down for one big reason. I wanted to transform the Varricchio name. I already thought of Sandy and Joe as my parents. I didn't need adoption papers to prove anything. More importantly, such documents would take away the only original identity I had left. In South Florida, the Varricchio's were known for illicit activities. People didn't respect us. They thought our family lacked moral fiber. I didn't like that. I wanted my father's name to be seen in a legitimate, positive light. I wanted to re-establish our family name, returning its rightful prestige.

Speaking about perception, aside from a couple fist fights—one of which I desperately tried to avoid—I completed middle school with surprising success. My grades continually improved and I even finished eighth grade on the Principal's Honor Roll. Things were definitely looking up as I headed into high school. I largely credit this to Sandy and Joe's positive influence and my desire to prove I wasn't just a screw-up.

Perhaps what I remember most about high school was the universal, desperate need to fit in with the crowd. Interestingly, there weren't many kids with my same background so it was difficult to imagine pretending to be someone else. Most kids I knew had fond memories of sleepovers, camping trips, family vacations, and birthday parties. My memories were far from the normal experiences of my peers. Still, I didn't let this get to me. I embraced my past and for the first time in my life, I was content just being myself.

Even so, for the most part, I kept my criminal record and ensuing incarcerations to myself. Some of my closer friends knew I was a foster child, but that was the extent of their knowledge. I tried to define myself through socially accepted activities instead. I tried out for several teams my freshman year, including cross-country, wrestling, and baseball.

I didn't last too long in cross-country because I had already spent most of my childhood running multiple miles every day and I was over it. Wrestling was a great outlet for aggression, but I wasn't keen on watching my weight during my formative years. For me, baseball was *the* sport. I loved the game and worked hard to improve my skills. Unfortunately, I wasn't a natural athlete and I had a much later start so I was behind the curve (pun somewhat intended). Despite my deficient skillset, I tried out for the high school team my freshman year. I was promptly cut. That sucked, but I knew I had work to do so I signed up for the local recreation-level team. I didn't care about the reputation; I just wanted to play.

Good things started to happen as high school went on. I began playing center-field and my agility and speed grew. If a ball was hit in the gap, I was on it in a hurry, earning playing time with my defensive skills.

Incidentally, as my defense improved, so, too, did my hitting. The thing that finally clicked for me was when a coach told me to "relax and focus on swinging easier." All these years, I thought it was most important to swing as hard as I could to drive the ball; however just the opposite proved to be true. I worked on swinging easier, employing about 80% of my normal effort. The results were exceptional. I went from batting last on every team to hitting in the two and three spots and being amongst the team leaders in hitting. Most importantly, I enjoyed the game. Just like in academics, my hard work and perseverance were paying off.

The following school year, I tried out for the high school team again. At that time, our high school only had one team: varsity. There was no junior varsity and no freshman team like there are nowadays. Though I knew the odds were against me, I was determined to play baseball for my high school and thus went through the lengthy tryouts once again.

While setting baseball goals, I also caught the acting bug and wanted to see how I might fare if I tried out for the high school musical. Although I had been in a couple small productions for my church (think Angel #5 in the back row of the annual Christmas play), I had practically no experience acting. Nonetheless, I had much practice pretending to be someone else to get what I wanted. In order to make my ambition come to life, I studied some lines, learned to sing a song, and even practiced dance moves the choreographer offered on the weekends and after school, prior to the auditions.

As I shuttled between baseball and musical tryouts, I happily enjoyed a bit of success at both. I was told by some of the baseball coaches my game had improved tremendously from the prior year and I had a real chance to make the team as a bench player. *Hot damn!* I couldn't believe it. I was possibly going to be on the baseball team. This was exciting.

After receiving the good news, I auditioned for the high school musical the next day. The feeling of being rooted onstage calmed me. Other people get nervous performing to crowds. Not me. Perhaps it had something to do with learning to project confidence in order to subsist in the Juvie pecking order, but I was fearless about public performances. After doing my scene, I learned the cast list would be posted just before lunch on the doors to the theater. I thought I did okay, but I wasn't sure exactly what to expect.

The next day, I walked to the theater at the posted time. As I approached, I saw a large group of about 25-30 kids hovering together, reading the cast list. They were hopping over each other's shoulders to get a clearer view of the names. I walked closer, anxious, as students one-by-one turned to walk away. Some were smiling, others were in tears as they left the group. I was just within sight of the list when someone slapped me on the back.

"Congrats, Kurt," a pretty sophomore told me. "That's awesome."

"Thanks," I cautiously replied, wondering what she meant.

At last, I reached the cast list and scanned the right column. I dragged my finger to the left of my name: 'Kurt Varricchio .... Arab."

Sweet! I landed a good role as one of the main Jets characters in *West Side Story*. I was definitely excited, but I had to contemplate this opportunity in light of the *possibility* of making the baseball team as a reserve player. I continued reading the cast list, wanting to see who else would be in the musical with me. Then, I saw my name a second time.

"What the heck is an understudy?" I asked aloud.

"It means you're the backup if the first guy is out," explained the person beside me.

"So, if this guy can't perform or quits the play, I take his part?"

"Yep, and it looks like you're the understudy for Riff— a lead role. Congrats."

Wow. So, not only did I receive a decent role in my very first audition, there was a chance I could play the main role, too. Of course, I didn't want the other guy to get sick or quit because I looked up to that kid a great deal. He was a senior with a great work ethic and lots of talent. The fact that I was next in line, though, boosted my confidence. My decision was made. I said goodbye to high school baseball and hello to theater and the performing arts. While I certainly missed playing baseball, this critical decision served me well in high school, college, and beyond.

Chapter Thirty-Four: Higher Education

High school was a major time of growth for me as it is with many people. After that first play, I continued my involvement in theater arts, eventually holding several leading roles throughout my last three years. The stage offered me a way to freely build new reputations. I always took my roles seriously because I never wanted to look bad in front of audiences. Here is where I learned to put effort, time, and energy into a valuable skill set. It's also where I discovered the true definition of commitment.

Very much like baseball, theater relies on the importance of teamwork.

A theatrical production requires a comprehensive effort from every individual. From the lead actors, to the ensemble, to the choreographer, to the stage and lighting crew, everyone needs to be on the same page to produce a seamless show. By the time I finished high school, I had fulfilled many leading roles, but understood it was a collaboration from everyone in the cast and crew that ultimately made a production successful.

In addition to being involved in the performing arts, I also remained heavily vested in student government and community service, as well as academics. I sometimes wondered what guys from my past, like Jerome or Jamie, might say if they saw me now. Miles away from my Baby

Gator persona, I served as class officer, club officer for multiple on-campus groups, and even coordinated a couple of community service projects for at-risk youth.

Just as in my middle school years, Sandy and Joe continued to provide me the emotional support, as well as tangible opportunities to do meaningful activities during this period of my life. Long ago, I tired of getting in trouble. Back in the old days, every time they threw me in Juvie, I promised myself I would turn my life around—that I would do things better. However, it wasn't until I received my foster parents' support, coupled with my own internal commitment to improve myself, that I finally broke the destructive cycle.

As I began to understand myself better, it became clearer to me I needed creative outlets to stimulate my overactive brain. I found that by keeping myself busy and involved, I could perform better academically because my emphasis wasn't on just the *quantity* of my studies, but rather on the *quality* of those studies. Eventually, I graduated high school with a 4.0 (weighted) grade point average, placing me in the top 5% of my graduating class. Based on this success, I received a scholarship to Florida State University. Plus, as a foster child, I was considered a ward of the court, so I received a full financial aid package.

I was proud of how I fared in school. I was a far cry from the kid who used to skip school to rob cars and break into houses. In addition to being the only one in my family to graduate high school, I knew academic success was creating opportunities for me. It was something nobody could take away from me. My foster parents continually emphasized learning because they wanted me to experience "a new normal." That is, they wanted me to embrace the challenges of education, using them as tools to enjoy success later in life.

Arriving on the Florida State University campus, I knew I had to accomplish two things over the next four years. First, I needed to focus on my academics, proving I belonged there. The vast majority of foster kids I knew never attended a university, much less graduated, so I wanted to demonstrate it was a real possibility for those at-risk, like me. It might not make sense to someone not carrying around this stigma, but it was a burden—and opportunity—I carried with me throughout my academic career. Something inside continued to propel me. I just knew I couldn't fail. Similar to how I was determined to reinvent the Varricchio name, I knew I had to be a positive role model for other kids with backgrounds like me.

Second, I wanted to be more than just a number on campus, so I threw myself into extracurricular activities. Aside from being referred to as a literal number throughout my troublesome childhood (inmate number, case number, etc.), I believed involving myself with various groups and activities would provide me much-needed balance. It was critical to use these opportunities to work on my social and emotional growth, so I continued to stick my nose under various tents before finding myself actually *inside* the tent.

At the beginning of my second semester at FSU, I pledged a fraternity, Sigma Phi Epsilon ("Sig Ep"). My fraternity brothers came from all over the country, from all different backgrounds, and I spent three and a half years getting to know them. While we had some brothers who were more interested in the traditional fraternity party lifestyle, the vast majority of us Florida State Sig Eps were intelligent, active, and eager.

The Florida State Sig Eps were involved throughout campus. From college athletes to star performers in theater, music, film and radio; from the Student Body President to various Student Senators; from leaders in Campus Crusade for Christ to members of the Annual Homecoming Court, Sig Eps were well-represented throughout Florida State University. This was not by accident.

At Sig Ep, our goal was to be recognized as FSU's *Fraternity of the Year*. In order to accomplish this, we needed to be a well-rounded organization permeating campus. Not only were Sig Eps expected to participate in the chapter's activities (philanthropies, intramural athletics, socials, etc.), each Sig Ep was also expected to engage in extra-curricular activities outside of the fraternity (collegiate athletics, student government, alumni relations and the like). More importantly, Sig Eps were expected to lead in the classroom.

While, understandably, many people scoff at the idea of a fraternity being anything other than a social outlet, I wasn't looking for another reason to party in college. As anyone who knows me can attest, I did okay for myself on the social scene. Instead, college was my big opportunity, and I wanted to find a group of stand-up gentlemen to share my ambitions with. The adage, "work hard, play hard" best describes these formative years for me.

Incidentally, my entire Sig Ep experience was nearly derailed when I was presented with a seductive temptation. Prior to the beginning of each school year, fraternities engage in a process known as "Rush." Its purpose is to recruit new fraternity members. In an effort to impress, fraternities often throw lavish, themed parties at their respective houses every weeknight, luring recruits to sign at tables staffed by attractive women.

I participated in Rush during my first week at FSU. During the process, I met with several fraternities, hobnobbing with interesting, entertaining people. Although I had no real intention of pledging a fraternity just yet, I wanted to visit each house and check out the social scene. During my visits, several fraternities were interested in recruiting me, however, one particular fraternity was especially aggressive in their pursuit.

Their house was located in a great spot—close to some nightclubs and the football stadium. The guys inside followed up with me after the first night, offering to bring me to the next evening's events. They bought me dinner, introducing me to all of the other guys, really stepping up their recruiting game. On the final night of Rush, it was time to make a decision. I was in a room with the President, Vice President of Recruitment, the Pledge Chair, and a couple other members. I knew this moment was coming and was prepared to accept their bid even though I came into this process not intending to join.

"Kurt," The VP of Recruitment started. "We have been impressed by your diligence and interest in our fraternity and think—"

My mind began to wonder. I questioned whether I gave myself enough time to process this decision. *Did I truly believe this was the right fraternity for me? Although these guys showed the most interest, was there another option if I waited until the following semester? Did I really want to take on another large commitment my very first semester?* Questions like these made we wonder what I was doing as they made their closing argument.

"Do you accept our bid?" asked the VP.

"You know guys," I said as if I had been in this situation a hundred times before. "While I appreciate your interest and all you've done, I don't think the time is right for me to commit."

I decided at that moment to wait one more semester so I could observe how these fraternities acted when the stage lights were off. I had been allured by misrepresentations in the past and I didn't want to allow my college career to begin the same way.

"Thank you again, and I'll be back in the spring to revisit," I told them. Members of the fraternity were surprised, but in hindsight, I am grateful I pumped the brakes on that decision. As it turns out, that fraternity was far from a good fit. During that first semester, I discovered many things I considered deficient about that fraternity that made me glad I never joined. Had I not relied on my past experiences and intuition to process the totality of this particular situation, my life would have turned out much differently. After all, later on, one of my brothers (from Sig Ep, my eventual fraternity) would end up introducing me to my future wife. I think I made the right decision.

Chapter Thirty-Five: Backslide to Criminality

In the summer of 1990, I failed to employ much of the critical thinking I had used ever since changing my life for the better. Everything I had worked so hard for was nearly derailed because of one of the worst decisions of my life. Perhaps even more disheartening than the decision itself was what I used to justify my actions. I foolishly allowed superficial influences to pervert my otherwise rational thinking. Although my foster parents had instilled values in me, I screwed up. I had a momentary lapse in judgment.

During the summer following my first year at college, I worked at a large department store, thanks to a family friend who stuck her neck out for me. I was an associate in the men's section, and fairly successful at upselling customers and securing sales. Another close friend of mine also worked in a separate department at the same store. We hung out all the time, at college and back in Fort Lauderdale. For some dumb reason, the two of us decided to take advantage of the store by concocting a criminal scheme.

It involved manipulation of inventory and purchases in two primary ways. The first part had to do with customers who would be "refunded" all or most of their purchase in cash. When a customer paid this way, we provided him or her a copy of their receipt. Back then, receipts were printed in triplicate: a white copy, a pink copy and a yellow copy. The store kept the white copy, the customer received the yellow copy, and the sales associate kept the pink copy for computing their commission.

Our scam worked like this: whenever a customer paid in cash, we would provide the cash-paying customer with the wrong receipt copy so they would get the pink copy and we would keep the yellow. We would hold onto the original receipt for a week or so, then issue a "return refund" for most of the items by using a "runner." In turn—and depending on who the runner was—we would keep a large portion of the proceeds, providing the runner with a fee for their services.

The second scheme we came up with involved adding items to our friends' purchases that were never paid for by the customer. For example, if one of our friends came in to purchase a pair of shorts and a t-shirt, we would add a couple of additional shirts, pants, and shorts to their bags. The deal was they would receive our employee discount and an additional item for free in exchange for securing the additional items for us.

While things started slowly, greed soon set in and we began scheming at a frenetic pace. Of course, it didn't take long for the authorities to catch on. A few weeks before we were scheduled to head back to college, my buddy and I were called into the store's Loss Prevention Department and forced to confess to our wrongdoing. As we were transported to jail, I recalled my days in juvenile hall. I had an idea of what to expect so I provided my friend with some information and guidance as we sat in back of the squad car.

"We stay together, hip-to-hip, once we get in there," I explained, "We're stronger as a pair than on our own. Do you understand?"

With his eyes full of apprehension and fear, he nodded my way.

"I mean it," I told him. "These people will take advantage of you in a hurry, so don't separate."

"Okay, okay. I got it. We'll stay together."

"One more thing. Don't act scared. Act like you've been there before."

He looked out the window again, every breath more ragged than the last. I wanted to slap him into straightening up. He couldn't act like that in there.

After processing, we were placed in a small jail cell with about ten other individuals. A bench ran along the right side of the wall, wrapping around to the left in an L-shape. In the back-left corner sat a small, metal toilet. It felt like déjà vu from my Juvie days. If you needed to use the bathroom, all eyes were on you—no privacy at all.

The following morning, they released us on bail. We quickly secured criminal defense attorneys to mitigate our sentences. While I feared the consequences, I also felt a kind of relief. I had come so far from my old days, yet things had gotten out of control. The scheme was bad enough, even worse were the reasons behind it.

For years, my foster parents provided me with everything I needed, and then some. During my first year of college, I discovered my fellow students had more than me: nice cars, great clothes, high-end electronics. Of course, I didn't need these items, but I *wanted* them; I felt they would command respect from my peers. This warped my thinking. I thought these things would elevate my stature. Instead, they nearly cost me everything I had worked so hard for.

Eventually, my defense attorney secured a plea deal, but the police pegged me as the brains behind the operation since I was the one with the criminal history. While I did participate, it wasn't my initial idea, nor was it my intention to take it as far as we did. The truth was my friend and I were young and dumb, and we just continued to get greedier.

Not that it matters much, but I actually began to feel guilty and stopped the activity two weeks prior to being arrested. I knew what I did was wrong and it ate at me inside. I wanted to disclose our activities to the store but was fearful of what might happen. Despite my guilt, I was on the defensive when word came out I concocted the whole scheme. It bothered me to be automatically suspected as the ring-leader due to my past. Of course, in retrospect, it makes sense the police pinned the entire operation-planning on me, but it still doesn't make it any easier to digest.

This experience taught me something valuable about judging people's characters, especially individuals like me, who were once punished for wrongdoing. Today, I try to reserve judgment until I have a total review of the facts and circumstances in any given situation. This is especially true with my kids when they ever veer off track.

Although we spent the night in jail, the worst was yet to come. Informing Sandy and Joe of this transgression was one of the most difficult things I have ever had to do. I felt like I stabbed them in the back. They had sacrificed so much for me and I had let greed cloud my judgment. It was convenient that they were out of town on vacation when I was arrested because I knew I couldn't even muster up the courage to speak to them in person. I wrote a letter. Joe was shocked and angry. Sandy just cried, which made me feel even worse.

Eventually, I returned to college to continue my education but had to keep my nose clean, maintain a certain grade point average, perform several hours of community service, and reimburse the department store. I was grateful my life wasn't ruined, but the fact I compromised my integrity for short-term superficial gain did not sit well with me. It was the last legal transgression of my life and, in true fashion, I used the negative experience as a learning opportunity.

Chapter Thirty-Six: Introduction to Scouting

I eventually graduated from Florida State University with a Bachelor of Arts in Media Performance (Broadcast Journalism), then continued my education at the University of Texas-Austin (UT) to pursue a Master's Degree in Sports Administration. As usual, I tried to get involved with as many things as possible at UT. I served as a Resident Scholar for my fraternity. I worked for the Athletics Department in various capacities, often for free to gain experience. Thanks to two of my professors, I was eventually hired as a Graduate Assistant for the UT Department of Kinesiology, assisting them with teaching several courses including *Sports Law, Sports Marketing* and *Facilities Management.*

In the Spring of 1995, I finished all of the required coursework for my Master's Degree but had one very important item left to complete: an internship. With assistance from one of my professors, I secured one with the Kansas City Chiefs in their promotions and marketing department. This was a crucial opportunity to learn from one of the best marketing departments in professional sports.

As an intern in their marketing department, the Chiefs provided me numerous opportunities to participate in their overall marketing plan. From coordinating point-ofsale promotions with major corporate sponsors, to ensuring athletes were appropriately involved with marketing deals for our corporate sponsors, I was given wide latitude and responsibilities. Because the Chiefs were willing to grant me these responsibilities, coupled with the fact my professor provided her endorsement to get me the internship, I was determined to prove my value. In the summer of 1995, I made my final presentation to the professors at UT, receiving my Master's Degree. The Chiefs hired me for the 1995 season and I began working in their Marketing and Promotions Department—the beginning of my professional career. At the time, I reflected back on that ride with my social worker in Tampa—past the Buccaneers Stadium on the way to the Butlers. I couldn't believe how far I'd come since then.

The Chiefs' 1995 season ended with an upset loss at home in the NFL Playoffs to Jim Harbaugh and the Indianapolis Colts. Although the Chiefs kept me onboard for the 1995 season, there were no guarantees beyond that year so I quickly moved into game-plan mode. I loved being a part of the Chiefs organization but I needed to search for the next logical step in my career development.

During my time with the Chiefs, I made a habit of getting to know as many people from as many departments as possible. I would often workout in the Chiefs complex (after the players did) where I met several coaches and scouts. Herman "Herm" Edwards was—and still is—one of my favorite people of all time. His energy, charisma, and willingness to engage in conversation with anyone is a truly unique attribute, and I knew he would be successful in whatever he decided to do.

In one of my conversations with Herm, we discussed scouting and the NFL Draft. I wanted to know what he was looking for in prospective players and how to determine if one was a good fit. He suggested I go to the scouting department to see if I could accompany a scout on a local trip. I did just that and, to my surprise, I was invited to accompany a scout to the University of Missouri during a September game. While the University of Missouri's roster was considered to be better than Northeast Louisiana's roster, the best player on the field was a speedy wide receiver for Northeast Louisiana who immediately caught my eye.

"Check out that wide receiver," I said to the scout. "He might be the fastest guy on the field."

"Yeah, he's fast," the scout said. "But the question is whether or not he can translate that speed into the game. Also, look how he catches punts high on his pads. If he does that, he won't be returning kicks in the NFL."

The scout went on to explain what to look for in terms of an offensive lineman, defensive lineman, and long snapper. I realized the breadth of an NFL scouting department and the importance of looking deeper into each athlete's overall abilities and tendencies. I would eventually learn the personal and emotional evaluation of a player is as equally important as their athletic skills.

During the Chiefs' 1995 season, I continued to poke my head into the scouting department. Once the season ended, I immediately asked about an opportunity. I understood my deficiencies in scouting, yet I was willing to do whatever they wanted me to.

Fortunately, the Chiefs provided a temporary opportunity and I spent the days leading up to the 1996 NFL Draft inputting scouting reports on thousands of players. It wasn't the most glamorous job, but it kept my foot in the business, allowing me to learn a great deal just by reading reports from the professional scouts. Incidentally, while inputting scouting reports, I recognized one player with four or five reports from different scouts. That player was a speedy wide-receiver from Northeast Louisiana, the same one I noticed on my scouting trip to Missouri: Stepfret Williams. Williams was eventually drafted by the Dallas Cowboys in the 3rd Round of the 1996 NFL Draft. I guess his speed played well enough to give him a shot at an NFL career. However, getting the opportunity is half the battle; taking advantage of that opportunity is something entirely different. This formidable experience helped me understand my ability in recognizing raw talent, a skill I would one day hone as an agent in my own right. In spite of life's setbacks, I was beginning to come into my own professionally.

Chapter Thirty-Seven: A Gutsy Phone Call

While I appreciated the opportunity to work for the Chiefs Scouting Department, I needed a more permanent opportunity so every day I sent letters and resumes all over the country. Every NFL team received a letter and resume. Every Major League Baseball team received a letter and resume. Every NBA team received a letter and resume. Approximately half of the NHL teams received a letter and resume. (I didn't understand hockey at the time so I stuck with those teams located in the United States.) Sports agencies large and small received letters and resumes. The USOC and its affiliate members received letters and resumes. The NCAA, NCAA Conferences and a number of universities all received cover letters and resumes.

I sent 250 letters and resumes all over the country as I continued my career search in late 1995. Unfortunately, the responses were virtually the same: "Thank you for your interest in (insert organization name), but we don't have any current opportunities." Or: "While your credentials are exceptional, we don't have any opportunities available at this time."

Every day I reviewed my mail and every day I would receive multiple rejection letters. My frustration increased daily. I knew I had the right skill set to make an impact with an organization, yet no one would give me an opportunity. Of course, this happens all the time to people, but I got more and more discouraged as the process continued. After several months of rejection letters, I reached my limit. I just had a particularly challenging day at the Chiefs after losing several hours' worth of work when the computer crashed. I had bills stacking up, and I didn't want to reach out to my parents for help again. After all, I received my Master's Degree so I could make myself more marketable to employers. I didn't want to disappoint my parents by telling them I remained unemployed despite my academic credentials.

I employed a variation of an old adage: "If you don't like the direction in which your ship is sailing, you have to adjust your sails because you cannot adjust the wind." This is exactly what I did—I adjusted my sails. During my drive home from the office I promised myself if I received another rejection letter that day, I would pick up the phone and call the team, organization, or entity to convince them *why* they needed me. I wasn't going to sit idle any longer. I needed to do something different because I couldn't change the wind.

As fate would have it, I arrived home and found one single letter in my mailbox. It was from the San Diego Padres and contained the same standard rejection text. It so happens earlier that day, I had just read an article in a sports-related publication about the Padres' lack of ticket sales and how the team struggled to eclipse one million tickets sold in 1995. The Padres actually sold just over one million seats that year but ranked 13th out of 14 National League teams in attendance that season. In 1993 and 1994, they ranked dead last in the National League in terms of attendance. I saw an opportunity to engage in a conversation with Don Johnson, the Padres Vice President of Marketing.

That night, I picked up the phone and called the San Diego Padres. Having already been rejected by them, I saw nothing to lose. I was tired of waiting for my ship to come in, so I decided to row out to meet it.

The phone rang and the Padres' operator answered. "Thank you for calling the San Diego Padres. How may I direct your call?"

"Hi. Can I please speak with Don Johnson?"

"May I say who is calling?"

Crap. I needed to keep calm and act like I knew what I was doing. "Sure," I said, acting like Mr. Johnson and I were old friends. "My name is Kurt Varricchio and I'm just reaching out to him to follow-up on his last communication to me."

"Please hold."

First obstacle down. But now I had a new problem: how was I going to start the conversation if Don Johnson actually picked up the phone? How would I handle his initial resistance and how could I fight through that resistance to get what I wanted—an opportunity?

With each pressing moment of doubt, I turned to my resolve, relying on experience. After all, I'd been through a hell of a lot worse situations and came out alive. I'd survive this.

Thirty seconds later, the operator returned. "Hi Kurt," she said sweetly, "Mr. Johnson is not available now. Would you like to leave a voicemail?"

"Sure, that would be great. Thank you."

With that, I left a short, direct message for Mr. Johnson identifying who I was, why I was calling, and how I would take no more than five minutes of his time if he called me back. Unfortunately, I did not receive a call back from Mr. Johnson within 48 hours, so I called again. Again, I received his voicemail and, again, I left a quick voicemail message. After a few more attempts, I finally got Mr. Johnson on the phone.

I was ready. I gave my pitch with the Padres' article on attendance in front of me. "Hi, Mr. Johnson. I received the Padres' letter to me regarding the lack of an opportunity with the Padres, but I think you made a mistake."

Mr. Johnson was probably a bit taken aback, but as an accomplished professional, he certainly didn't show it. "What do you mean?"

"I'm looking at this article that says the Padres are struggling to sell tickets and I think I can help you." I couldn't believe I was saying something so brash, but then again, I had nothing to lose.

"Well, we don't have any marketing or corporate sales opportunities available right now."

Because I specifically requested a marketing and corporate sales position in my cover letter to the Padres, I had to quickly shift my sails to get through Mr. Johnson's wind resistance.

"Okay," I said quickly. "If that's the case, perhaps there's something I *can* do to help you sell tickets in some other capacity. I can assure you, Mr. Johnson, I will make you a lot more money than you will pay me and I know I can help increase attendance." I paused, then made the final push. "All I want is an opportunity and I will make sure I'm worth the risk, sir. I saw the Padres barely sold one million tickets last year and I know I can help you sell more."

"Okay." Mr. Johnson's tone lightened. "I would like you to speak with our Director of Sales, Louie Ruvane. He handles season tickets, group sales, and skybox sales. Would you be interested in that?"

You bet your ass I'm interested in sales. "Sure. I would definitely be interested in helping the Padres fill seats and I'm willing to do whatever it takes."

"Great. I'm going to have Louie Ruvane contact you."

As I hung up, I asked myself why I didn't do something like this earlier. I realized taking a risk could be fruitful, especially when there was nothing to lose. Had my conversation with Mr. Johnson gone awry, I would still be in the same position I was when I called him. If, however, I could convince him to provide me an opportunity, then I just turned a negative (rejection) into a positive (a job interview).

After several weeks, I finally spoke with Louie Ruvane. Louie was a polished salesman with a knack for management and had a track record of success with Major League teams. He initially spoke with me on the phone, then invited me out for an interview. I made the trip to San Diego, met with Louie and several other members from the ticket office, and secured my first full-time opportunity in professional sports.

While the opportunity to work in professional baseball was exciting, the starting salary was less than desirable. I was offered $20,000 per year, plus commission. Living in San Diego on $20,000 per year seemed impossible, especially in the face of outstanding student loans for graduate school. But, like a good salesman, Louie explained I could make more money based on how they structured commission. Apparently, the starting salary was similar to a score card in golf. Everyone was at different levels in their careers (just as golfers have different levels of abilities) but they were doing what they wanted. If you played golf more, your score would get better. Likewise, if you worked more, your salary and commission would improve.

Louie was right. I accepted the opportunity after a lot of number crunching and budget planning. I figured if I could make $5,000 in commission for the year, I could survive. If I could get the results I wanted, I would receive the pay I wanted. Just like the old days, trying to do everything I could to survive, I was relentless. I chased the dangling carrot from the first day and my efforts yielded exceptional results. I wound up more than doubling my salary that year with commissions and bonuses. Not only did I get my foot in the door, I was doing what I loved with a group of dynamic, motivated, and hungry coworkers—all of whom had made a lasting impact on my life. I'm grateful I decided to make that phone call and if you're reading this book, I encourage you to take whatever calculated risk you're contemplating today. You at least owe it to yourself to try.

Chapter Thirty-Eight: Amy

The 1996 World Series pitted the Atlanta Braves against the New York Yankees. I was in charge of taking The Big Hitters—a group of community businessmen and women who helped the Padres sell tickets—to the game as a way of saying thank you. Right before the trip, I received a fortuitous phone call from a fraternity brother and good friend, Todd "Boodah" Markel.

"You gotta meet my cousin who goes to San Diego State," Boodah said.

"Yeah. Why's that?"

"Because she's good looking. And single. And in a sorority at SDSU." He instantly checked my three boxes. "Now come down and meet her, you tool."

As soon as I said I would, Boodah made plans for all of us to go to the Monday Night Football game between the Raiders and the Chargers, scheduled for October 21, 1996. This was shaping up to be an epic weekend of sports. I was scheduled to see Game 1 of the World Series in New York on October 19th, Game 2 of the World Series on October 20th, then Monday Night Football in San Diego on October 21st.

As it turned out, Game 1 was postponed from the 19th to the 20th because of rain and Game 2 was moved to Monday night. Since our group already had flights booked, we decided to leave New York after only seeing Game 1 of the World Series (a 12-1 victory by the Braves). Even after one game, we were all so exhausted the last thing I wanted to do was go to another sporting event. As soon as we landed in San Diego, I called Boodah.

"I'm sorry, but I'm out for this game. I need to get some sleep."

"Fine, but you gotta meet her, Kurt. Come to the bar after the game?"

I paused, looking longingly at my clean, made bed.

"Trust me Kurt. Come on…"

"Fine. I'll take a nap now and meet you at the bar later."

The three of us met around 10:00 pm that evening. I entered the small bar off El Cajon Boulevard and immediately noticed a beautiful blonde standing beside Boodah.

"This is my cousin, Amy," the matchmaker said proudly. "Amy, this is my fraternity brother, Kurt."

Amy and I shook hands. I tried to play it cool. "Nice to meet you Amy. I heard a lot of good things about you."

Ugh! Such a lame line.

"Nice to meet you too. I also heard a lot about you."

Okay, cool. Her line is just as corny.

I then turned to Boodah to give him the obligatory bro-hug. "Good to see you, Boodah."

"You too, Chio. Glad you could make it." (Chio was my nickname from college. I guess people got tired of trying to say Varricchio, so they adjusted accordingly.)

After momentarily engaging Boodah, I returned my attention to his beautiful cousin. I smiled. She knew the required small-talk pleasantries so she made them into statements instead of questions. Even within our brief conversation that night, I noticed something very different about Amy—she was assertive, smart, athletic, outgoing, and definitely a looker.

Our conversation continued until Amy issued me a challenge. "Do you want to play *Foosball?*"

"Sure, but I gotta tell you that I'm not that good so don't judge."

We all laughed, then made our way to the table. Amy dropped the ball in and promptly began kicking my butt. To this day, I always tell her that I allowed her to win as a gentleman, but she rolls her eyes since she knows the real deal.

After spending a few hours together, we said our goodbyes and I told her I would call her later in the week. Trying to play it cool, I handed her my Padres business card before we shook hands and walked away for the evening. I went home and immediately called the girl I was casually dating to break it off. I knew Amy was the right person for me and I cautiously hoped she felt the same.

While I fell for Amy quickly, the first few months of our relationship filled me with anxiety. *Could I disclose everything about my past to her? Would she accept my childhood criminal history or turn away?* I had to be strategic. I had to come clean early. I thought Amy was the perfect girl to spend the rest of my life with and I certainly couldn't ask for her emotional investment without telling her the truth.

I decided to do it one evening after we went for a run together. The endorphins gave me courage. I was going to go home, cook us dinner, then lay it all out on the kitchen table. My hands shook as I drained the pasta, whisking the pesto sauce. She sat on the couch in the living room with no idea what was coming. I washed my hands, took a deep breath, and walked in the room.

"How's dinner coming?"

"Fine."

She looked so beautiful just sipping her water bottle, wiping little beads of sweat from her forehead. When she smiled at me, I returned it nervously.

"Something wrong?" she asked.

I knelt beside her and took her hands. "I grew up with three older brothers, a baby sister, and a mom. I never knew when I was going to eat. My brothers beat me up nearly every day..."

I had never told anyone the things I told her but I didn't leave anything out. Not even the worst stuff. Before long, I got choked up. It bothered me to let her see me this way, the tears sliding down my face, yet I did it anyway.

Instead of running for the door, she took my hands, squeezing them as I struggled through the hardest parts. Before long, she was crying too.

"I was so worried you would think less of me," I said.

She dabbed her eyes. "I'm shocked. I'm angry. No child should be treated this way. But I'm on your side, Kurt. And always will be."

She kissed me. That moment was the beginning of a trusted friendship. Amy and I came from vastly different upbringings, but she never judged me. We couldn't fit more perfectly as a couple.

Two years later, we married with Boodah as the prideful best man taking credit for everything, of course. Looking back on our fateful meeting in October 1996, I realize, once again, stepping outside of my comfort zone had yielded exceptional results. It would have been easy to blow off Boodah due to travel exhaustion. If I did that it could have cost me my wife. Sure, Amy and I might have met in a different way, but then again, we might have not.

I can't imagine not having this incredible woman at the center of my life.

Chapter Thirty-Nine: Fortune Calls

Three weeks after Amy and I were married in Dana Point, California, I started law school at the University of San Diego (USD). I was still working full-time for the Padres, so I took evening classes part-time. The difference between a full-time law student and a part-time law student was simply one class. During my first year of law school, I took four classes each semester, Monday through Thursday. It was a grind.

After my first semester of law school in December of 1998, Amy and I decided it would be best if I quit the Padres and went to school full-time. I was constantly in an over-time state and Amy and I missed being together. But in December of 1998, fate made another decision for us: we learned Amy was pregnant with our first son, Corbin. I had to keep working for the Padres, but I continued pursuing my law degree.

After the first year of law school, I made my own schedule: I took a morning class, went to work for a few hours, took a couple more afternoon classes, then returned to the Padres to work during game times. Although time seemed to stand against me, I managed to juggle it all, using skills from my past and focusing on the end game plan. Amy helped me manage it all when necessary, and I had her support throughout the entire process.

While Amy was not quite a risk taker like me, she trusted my judgment, and balanced me out with sound reasoning. I wasn't afraid to jump, and she wasn't afraid to soften the blow if I fell. Amy and I also shared many similarities. Though we grew up in extremely different environments, we both shared an affinity for helping those in need. In January of 1999, this shared trait ended up giving us a personal gain.

While in the sales office, a young lady called me, wanting to purchase tickets for her father as a birthday gift. In my department, I only sold season tickets, skyboxes, and deals for corporate groups. I assumed she was looking for season tickets so I offered her a pair of seats in the Padres Club Level, which required a minimum 40-game purchase.

She was taken aback by the four-figure cost. "I can't afford that much," she said, deflated. "I was just hoping to get about five or six games for him."

"Oh, okay. Well, this area is for half-season and full-season ticket sales only. The smaller plans are going to be located in the outfield or view level. Do you want me to look there?"

"I don't know. He really wanted to sit in the club infield section. I'm sorry, I know this is your job. I just... he can't afford tickets himself so I wanted to surprise him with really great seats. He has done so much for me and I wanted to do something special for him. He's such a huge Padres fan."

I could tell she was being genuine and her words struck a chord with me. That's easily how I could have described my own father, Joe. "Tell you what," I said. "I think we have some in-house seats available but I need to confirm it. Can you hold for a few minutes?"

Excitement returned to her voice. "Yes."

I relayed the story to my supervisor and asked if we could sell a couple special seats to her, just for a few games. He said yes. I picked up the phone, relieved I didn't have to formulate an apology. "Your Dad's gonna be a happy man."

"Really?" I could feel her smile through the phone. "Oh, thank you so much!"

"No problem. I admire the fact you want to do this for your dad. Now, just let me search these tickets for you. It'll take a minute." The page was buffering painfully slow so I decided to make conversation in the interim. "What do you do for a living?"

"I work for *Wheel of Fortune*."

"Really? That's awesome. How do you like it?"

"I love it. It's a great place to work."

"That's cool. So, I love that show. Do you mind if I ask a question?"

"Sure, go ahead." She knew where this was going as I'm sure she encountered this question daily.

"How do you get on it? Is there an audition?"

"Yeah. You first send in a card with your contact information. Once we get those, we call people in. Then, they have to pay their own way to get to the audition and there is a huge process for that. It's really several layers."

"How long does it typically take?"

"About six months or so to get a call for the audition." She paused for about 3-4 seconds, then added, "Unless, of course, *you know somebody*."

I took the cue. "Well, do I know somebody?"

"You do now."

I sat up straighter. "Seriously?"

"Yes, I'm serious. I appreciate you helping me with this and going above and beyond, so it's the least I can do."

"That's great. Thank you."

"My pleasure. Now, just so you know, I can get you into the audition ASAP, but I can't guarantee you'll get on the show. That all depends on how you do at the audition."

"Well, if you get me the audition, I will take care of the rest."

We both laughed. Two weeks later I auditioned for the show. To do so, I had to sacrifice one of my Property Law classes. Skipping class was especially frowned upon in the first year, but I had to jump at this once-in-a-lifetime opportunity. I told a couple of friends to keep it quiet, but of course, when the professor asked where I was, they thought it was too cool to stay silent.

"He's auditioning for the *Wheel of Fortune* in LA!"

I think the surprise of it all kept the professor from reprimanding me too harshly for my absence.

The first round of auditions included eighty people in a simulation game. The final round had one requirement: stand up in front of everyone and talk about yourself. Some people clearly shook with nerves, but I couldn't wait to stand up and blab. A week later, a producer called to congratulate me for making it on the show.

At the taping, we rehearsed the game, reviewed stage positioning, what to say and what not to say, and how to appropriately project our voice. I had been wanting to go on this show since I was twelve years old and couldn't believe I was about to see Vanna White directing me towards the board in person. Participating in the greatest show on TV (in my opinion), I knew I couldn't embarrass myself. I was determined to win. Amy and I were expecting a child in six months. I had to get that money to put toward a home. While I let myself enjoy the experience at first, my competitive side soon kicked in.

I only had a few hundred dollars in my *Fortune* account when it was my turn to spin during the "Star and Role" puzzle. I guessed a few letters, bought a vowel, then spun. I grabbed the wheel and gave it a twirl, my eyes shifting intermittently between the wheel and the board.

The wheel started to slow. It would either land on two bankruptcy silvers or the gold $10,000 sliver right in between. I held my breath, yet something told me this was going to be my moment. The wheel stopped. Right on the $10,000 gold sliver! The audience went crazy. So far, the puzzle had an M, C, D, two L, two G's, and four O's. I scrambled the letters in my mind, and suddenly I was on a lunchtime jog again, listening to my friend, Will. It clicked and I knew the answer.

Rewind three months. I was working out with a colleague of mine, Will Berry, from the Padres, on our lunch break. Will and I always talked about random things during our runs, but during this particular four-mile run, he entertained us both by talking about movies.

"So, do you and Amy plan on watching the *Oscars* this weekend?" Will asked as we completed the second mile of our run.

"I'm not sure what Amy has planned for us."

"I hear you on that one. Kimberly does the planning for us too." We both chuckled, then Will continued. "You know what my favorite actor and role is of all time?"

"No, what?"

"Michael Douglas playing Gordon Gekko in *Wall Street*."

"I never saw that," I panted. "Is it worth seeing?"

"It's one of the best movies and performances I've ever seen."

At the time of my appearance on *Wheel of Fortune,* I still hadn't seen the movie, but I somehow remembered our conversation. The funny thing? I wouldn't have been able to solve the puzzle if I hadn't gone for a run that day with Will.

After securing the letter "K", Pat Sajak asked me if I'd like to solve the puzzle.

"I'd love to solve the puzzle, Pat. *Michael Douglas as Gordon Gekko.*"

I won, receiving a chance at the Bonus Round. Minutes later, I stood with Pat and Vanna smiling encouragingly in front of me. The category was "thing," featuring a five-letter word. They provided R, S, T, L, N, and E, so I stood in front of "_ _ N E _."

Meanwhile, Pat asked me to select three more consonants and one vowel. "I'd like a...C, a D, an H, and an O," I said carefully.

Vanna touched each space, leaving me with "HONE_." I looked at the board, raising one eyebrow as this was too obvious. Amy stood in the audience and, although I wasn't able to look at her, I sensed she was smiling, incredulous at the irony. I referred to Amy as 'honey' more often than her real name, and her family and close friends always ribbed me about it.

"Honey," I said confidently, yet inquisitively. Pat responded, "Yes, thank you dear," as everyone laughed. My laughter quickly changed to exuberance as Pat told me my prize was an all-expense paid trip to Paris for four people.

Amy and I debated for weeks about which couple to invite. Once I told her we wouldn't have even received the trip to Paris without Will, we decided to invite him and his girlfriend at the time, Kimberly. Not only were they great travel partners, but Will actually spoke French—he had lived in France for about eight years when his dad worked for the US Government. We learned all of this *after* we extended the invitation. Amy and I felt this was almost too good to be true. Incredibly, Will knew Paris like his own backyard. Somehow, without even knowing it, we had acquired our own personal tour guide. Kimberly was also a great person to bring along and we had one of the most eventful vacations of our lives. Will and Kimberly would eventually marry, proving both Paris and *Wheel of Fortune* were definitely magical.

Chapter Forty: Do or Die

"Honey, I need to pass this bar exam in July or we're going to be behind the eight-ball big time."

"You'll be fine," Amy reassured me. "Just put the time in."

By 2002, we were both working and going to school. My wife was a school teacher taking additional classes to advance her career, and I was just about to finish law school while continuing to work for the Padres. I would graduate in May, then sit for the exam in July. The California Bar was considered one of the toughest in the country (a 50/50 chance of passing on the first time) and I needed to pass it on the first time. Why? Because on top of everything else, we were expecting our second son, Johnny, in the middle of the year so financial success became imperative.

It was late at night and neither of us could sleep so we had the television on. Though I hadn't yet disclosed my anxiety about the test to Amy as I continued to focus on my next move, I finally succumbed to the pressure and blurted out my concerns.

"What am I going to do, Amy? I have no time to study. If I don't pass the bar exam on the first try, we're screwed."

Amy's response was swift, her eyes shifting from the television screen to me. "Just go on another game show and win some money."

I raised my eyebrows. *That wasn't a bad idea.*

"You know what? I will. I'll start looking tomorrow."

Six weeks from that very conversation, I found myself sitting in a studio with Whoopi Goldberg, Bruce Vilanch, Marlee Matlin and Doris Roberts competing on *Hollywood Squares.* After a phone and in-person interview, I had somehow proved myself as a game-show personality. Though it was my second time on a game show, I was more nervous in this taping because I needed extra brain power. I knew I wouldn't know all the answers, and I didn't want to look dumb on national TV.

I spent the day going over stage positioning and projection with the crew just like we did on *Wheel of Fortune,* then we drew numbers. On *Squares,* the winner would proceed to the next day as the champion, taking on a new challenger. By the time my number was called, my female competitor had won four straight games and was playing for her fifth win—the maximum allowable limit. This girl was really rolling. *No pressure. It's not like I didn't have my whole future—and my family's finances—on the line.*

I took a deep breath before walking on stage. Accepting the challenge before me, I tried to remain calm beneath the barrage of questions from the host, Tom Davidson. Though I was visibly sweating under the hot lights as I struggled to formulate rapid-fire answers, I managed to dethrone the champion, claiming the title for myself.

Making it to the final bonus round, it was now time to choose my celebrity partner. Though I adored Whoopi Goldberg as an actress and comedian, my instincts propelled me toward Bruce Vilanch since I knew he knew more about celebrity gossip and the arts than me. My plan worked! We fired back right answer after right answer—

me answering those involving sports, geography and science—him nailing the music, literature, and history categories. We rocked the bonus round, racking up a whopping $18,000!

At the end of the bonus round, Tom Davidson turned to ask if I wanted to go "double or nothing" with a single bonus question. I was majorly tempted. After all, the category was sports. By then, though, I had learned a valuable lesson the hard way. If something sounded too good to be true, it probably was. Much to the audience's disappointment, I declined the offer.

Boy, am I glad I trusted my gut. Tom read the question, and I would've missed it. Over the course of two shows, I won over $23,000 and knew exactly what to do with it. Shortly after winning on *Hollywood Squares*, I told the Padres I was going to resign, effective May 31, 2002, to focus on my studies. Using my earnings from *Hollywood Squares*, coupled with my sales bonuses, Amy and I had enough money to allow me to fully commit to exam preparation.

Beginning on June 1st, Monday through Saturday followed the same routine. I attended prep courses in the morning, then drove to the University of California-San Diego Science Library to prepare for the afternoon and evening. I would eat lunch, go for a run on the beach, hose off at the science pier, then hit the books until about 6 or 7 o'clock each evening. After that I went home to spend time with the family before cracking the books again for a couple more hours. On Sundays, I studied for a few hours in the morning, then took the rest of the day off.

Fear of failure was my motivation. I had to pass on the first try for the sake of my family; there could be no other option. As the exam approached, I planned for every type of situation. Two of the most critical involved planning for traffic issues—the bane of existence for my fellow Southern Californians. Because we lived in Rancho Penasquitos, a San Diego suburb located a good distance from the testing site, I booked a hotel room a couple of miles from the exam location to save me the stress of morning traffic. I also brought my bicycle, placing it in my hotel room as a backup transportation mode. (A couple of years earlier, a large truck full of soup flipped over on the highway, blocking the route to the examination site. Several test takers were actually stuck in traffic and unable to complete the exam.) If something like that threatened to happen to me, I wanted to be ready. I felt like my ten-year-old hustler self again, strategizing, except this time I was trying to do something honorable for my family, instead of finagling an *Atari* game console.

Without going too far into the details about the test itself, I can say I satisfactorily stuck to my game plan (timing, strategy, etc.), passing my exam on the first try. I was excited, relieved and, most importantly, proud of the fact I triumphed for my family who sacrificed so much for me during those challenging summer months.

Chapter Forty-One: Ultimatum

Now that I passed the exam, it was time to find a job. Although I was working part-time as a law clerk for one of my former Big Hitters, I needed something of the more permanent variety. Since I had already spent my entire career in professional sports, I was not interested in simply being an attorney; I wanted to utilize my law degree to become a professional sports agent.

I entered the agent business for a few reasons. First, I thought it would be exciting to work with professional athletes, especially since I had already spent my entire career in the sports industry. Second, I wanted to help influence the influencers. From firsthand experience, I knew how kids looked up to athletes as role models. To me, it was important to make sure athletes also understood the impact their actions had on children. The more I could encourage clients to cultivate a positive image, both on and off the field, the greater positive effect they would have on others.

When my family and I first moved to Orange County, I supplemented my fledgling athlete firm with a job at a civil law firm. They agreed to let me nurture my athlete representation business on the side, so I took the attorney position, hoping the $75K/year salary would sustain us through mortgage payments and daycare. About six weeks in, I was still managing to keep all of the balls juggling in the air. Not only was I the top billing attorney in the firm, but I was actually picking up athlete clients. It was a grind, but it was working—until someone grabbed the third ball.

One morning as I was driving to the firm, I received a call from one of the partners, reminding me of a company-wide meeting that was to start in thirty minutes. At the time, I was fifteen minutes from the office. I told the partner I was on my way and would soon be there. She then started questioning why I was running an athlete representation firm on the side. I politely explained how I disclosed this fact during my interviewing process and that I always intended to build my other business as I worked as a lawyer. The main partner who started the firm had already agreed to allow this.

For some reason, this particular partner had a spur in her saddle that day and started to question the entire situation. "Your athlete firm is a distraction to other partners," she said testily.

"I'm sorry, I don't quite understand." I balanced the phone on speaker on my knee as I drove. "I informed the owner about my situation during the interview process, well before I was hired. We even discussed this in detail during the interview. With all due respect, I'm the highest billing attorney right now, so I don't see how my side endeavor is distracting the firm."

She still wasn't having it. "I've already talked to the other partners. You need to either drop the athlete representation firm or resign today."

Devastated, I immediately pulled over and called Amy. "So, I just got off the phone with one of the firm's partners," I said, choking back tears. "She said I have to either stop being an agent or quit the law firm."

"*What?*" Amy asked. I could hear the righteous anger in her voice. "They knew about your other business when you interviewed."

"Yeah, I know, but a couple of the younger partners don't agree with her decision and I have to pick one or the other."

Amy knew how important my dream was to me. "Well, what are you going to do?"

So many thoughts raced through my head; most involved Amy, Corbin, and Johnny. Others focused on my current athlete clients who were relying on me to help them—*I couldn't just abandon them, could I?* Yes, we desperately needed the steady income from the law firm, but I also desperately wanted to pursue my athlete representation business. "I think I have to keep the law firm job because we need the money, especially with the mortgage, daycare, law school loans, and other expenses." My throat was sore as I continued to hold back my tears.

"Sure. But what about your career goals and ambitions? What about all of the work you've already put into that?"

I left the phone on my knee, staring out the windshield at a rainy freeway, cars whizzing by my left side. "You know I'm a survivor. You know I'll find a way to make things work."

"Yes, I know and that's why I want you to call that firm back and tell them to go to hell."

I smiled, knowing I truly did marry my best friend. She understood who I was and what I wanted. Though the lack of a guaranteed salary obviously created anxiety, I had been through more stressful situations in my life and I was determined to get through this. I called the owner back and told her I was parting ways. The next week I opened

"The Law Offices of Kurt Varricchio." I haven't worked for anyone other than myself since.

Chapter Forty-Two: My Why

I choose to represent baseball players because baseball is a game of failure. It tests your perseverance and humility. Each player's individual performance is critical to the team's success so players must compartmentalize their failures and proceed toward the team goal—winning. Also, similar to life, baseball forces you to develop resiliency.

I kept such resiliency in mind when first trying to break into the sports industry—a seemingly impossible endeavor. Just as I did seven years earlier, at the time I sent out cover letters and resumes all over the country, searching for an agent job. Approaching the largest firms, right on down to the solo guys, I churned out resume after resume, seeking interviews.

I had no such luck so I expanded my search into other areas, reaching out to various universities and colleges, athletic conferences, the US Olympic Committee and other sports governing bodies. I was willing to relocate and go wherever the opportunity presented itself. My exhaustive search turned up nothing. Growing frustrated, I continued to work part-time as a law clerk in downtown San Diego. My frustration finally reached a peak when I received a call out of the blue from a good friend of mine over at the Padres.

"You still looking to represent athletes?" he asked.

I was sitting at my desk in front of unpaid bills when he called. "Of course. But I can't get an opportunity with a firm."

"Well I have a friend who was just released from the minor leagues. He doesn't have an agent yet. Wanna help him?"

Though I had no idea how I was going to do this, I leaped at the chance. The next day I called the ex-minor leaguer, explaining my experience was limited to working the front office for teams in the NFL and MLB. I was upfront. I told him he would be my first client, but that I would work my ass off to secure him an opportunity. I think he appreciated my candidness because within a few days, he signed a contract. With that, I officially became a sports agent.

Admittedly, I had little idea what I was doing at first, but I was committed to learning the business. I called all the Major League Baseball clubs, then went down the list of independent baseball leagues. I didn't fear rejection. When a club said they had no interest, I just moved onto the next.

My persistence paid off when I finally signed my client in the Canadian Baseball League, an independent entity comprised primarily of Rookie Ball and Low-A level players throughout Canada. Though it was a small win, it gave me the confidence I could actually make it as an agent, helping athletes breakthrough in their careers. With this opportunity, I knew things could (and would) escalate if I stuck to my game plan. Since that first small triumph, I have represented dozens and dozens of great guys. My favorite stories are the special interest ones—guys like me who overcame significant personal challenges to pursue their dreams.

One of my favorite such stories involved a client who persevered despite being abandoned by his parents during his teenage years. His mother left the family at an early age, leaving the father to care for their children. The father wasn't ready to deal with the stress, though. This created a tremendous amount of anxiety in the house. My client told me stories about how his dad would disappear for months at a time, leaving my client and his teenage siblings alone to fend for themselves. I could relate when he told me often times, his father didn't leave money or food, abandoning his children.

This abandonment created angst in my client. It also left deep emotional scars. Nonetheless, he found his outlet in high school athletics, discovering his exceptional abilities on the baseball diamond. Without any support system, he persevered through his high school years. His exceptional character and commitment pulled him through those tumultuous hard times. No matter what happened, he never gave up. Eventually, his efforts paid off and he was drafted by a Major League club, where he enjoyed a significant major league career. While this man understandably has trust issues with others, he and I share a common background, allowing us to connect on a deeper level.

Not only do I understand what my client went through and the scars it left, but I empathize with him. I help him see things from a different, sometimes more logical, perspective. As is common with people abandoned by their loved ones, the anger and spite they feel are real. Though most damaged individuals harboring such anger won't admit it, anger drives much of their decisions, influencing their behavior—both good and bad. How do I know this? The same thing happened with me.

It means a lot to me as an agent to be able to talk my clients off the ledge when facing difficult times—both on and off the field. They know they can turn to me when there is nobody else to turn to. The fact is, my industry is fraught with people whose only intention is to make as much money off a player as possible, then cast them aside once their career is on the downslope. Such a reality is frustrating to me because my intention is to build lifelong relationships with my clients by providing value. Not only do I strive to make my clients' careers better, I work to make their *overall lives* better through offering guidance, insight, and direction most people can't.

Providing value-added services, I rely on my personal and professional experiences to not only help my clients when they are in need, but also to teach them how they can help themselves. Along my journey, I have encountered numerous people who have added value to my life in one way or another. Their influence has been instrumental in the evolution of my own needs and, as such, I make it my objective to reciprocate.

When I was younger, my primary needs were food, shelter and safety, and each day was spent trying to meet those basic needs. Today, those primary needs are met so my focus has transcended to something more fulfilling: self-actualization. To me, self-actualization represents adding value to the lives of those individuals with whom I come in contact, especially my family, friends and clients. This is why I exist – to add value to other people's lives – and I am indiscriminate when it comes to *who* I choose to help.

I don't ever want my clients to feel as if I have abandoned them; whatever they need, they know they can come to me first. If I don't immediately have an answer, I will find the right people who do have an answer, and I will make sure those individuals are exceedingly qualified. This is my commitment to my clients and, as far as I'm concerned, there can be no exceptions. I have served the role of relationship counselor. I have provided guidance and direction on parenting and family issues. I have assisted clients in purchasing vehicles, investment properties and homes. I have even sat in a surgery center waiting room to provide moral support when my client had nobody else to comfort him. Whatever my clients' needs, I will be there. My specific life experiences shape my philosophy. Though I was left alone to fend for myself most of my life, my clients will never walk alone on their respective journeys. This is my commitment to them.

While all agents provide a similar "how" in terms of handling a player's career, what athletes should ask their prospective agents is "why" they do what they do. I truly believe I am where I am today for a reason. I believe that reason is to serve as an example for other kids who are in a similar situation I once was. As mentioned, most of the kids I hung out with during my early years are either incarcerated or dead. I have no doubt if I had remained in the situation I was in, I would have followed their same path.

Except for a handful of angels, like Barbara, Joe and Sandy, most adults in my youth largely wrote me off. They said I was a loser, that I wouldn't amount to anything or that I was destined to be incarcerated for life. Correctional officers, attorneys, neighbors, *even teachers*—all directly communicated these thoughts to me. Their negative opinions fueled my fire to prove them wrong.

People don't understand how impactful their words can be to a child, but they are significant. This is why I coached

20+ seasons of Little League baseball, several years of flag football, and remain active in my children's schools and activities. I want to make sure my kids and the kids with whom they interact, receive positive feedback and direction. Life isn't so much about *what* happens to us as it is about *how we react to what happens to us.* In particular, participation in youth sports aids in this developmental process. Teaching our children how to utilize these kinds of experiences for growth, beyond athletics, is one of the most important things we can do as parents, coaches, and mentors.

Along these same lines, I always remind my clients that everyone's road to the Big Leagues is different. For some, it takes three years, for others it can take eight, nine or more. One of the most important tips I can give to clients is to focus on what they *can* control. Things such as trades, other players' promotions, social media assassins, and front office shuffling are all aspects beyond their control. They shouldn't waste their time on those concerns. I ask my players to instead focus on what matters—to consider obstacles they've faced, and how they've overcome them. I also remind them of the process they learned from developing their baseball skills, and to find solutions within the game itself.

Today, the vast majority of my professional time is dedicated to athlete representation. I use the term "professional time" because I want to differentiate between the need to focus on one's career and the need to focus on one's family. If one's profession is the vehicle driving them through life, then family is the fuel that makes the vehicle run. Finding a delicate balance between family and career is of utmost importance. While I am proud of the professional accomplishments I've achieved, I'm prouder of the fact I've been heavily involved with my family throughout the journey. From coaching my sons' Little League baseball teams, to volunteering in their classrooms and at their schools, I've worked to strike a balance between being a good father and a good baseball agent. I don't think these two ideas are mutually exclusive. They are both necessary to achieve a balanced, healthy life.

Ultimately, there will be peaks and valleys in one's life. The peaks are the highlights of our lives, like the birth of a child, or marrying your best friend. The valleys are the low points, like a bad relationship or an "F" on a critical exam. Handling the peaks are easier because that's when things are at their best—you just have to remain humble and hungry. Aspire for more peaks and challenge yourself to continue the climb.

Dealing with the valleys, on the other hand, is entirely different. How an individual chooses to respond to valleys is what defines their character and ultimately leads them on the path to success. Ask yourself: do you choose to treat your valleys as an opportunity to learn for positive growth, or as an excuse to fail? It has been my observation throughout the years that those who chose valleys as motivation are the individuals who prove people wrong, who overcome obstacles more quickly. They won't back down. They stay committed to their goals despite setbacks.

Those, however, who use a valley as a reason to fail do not understand the impact of their flawed interpretation on a situation. During my troubled youth, I constantly heard criminals blame their plight on the valleys in their lives. These individuals conveniently made excuses as to why they were in their respective situations. Such thoughts are the products of a weak mind—one willing to give up because it's the easier route.

For those of you who have never used your valleys as motivation, I challenge you to shift your mindset. Use your obstacles as stepping stones rather than stumbling blocks. Everyone—*and I mean everyone*—has valleys in their lives. The difference between those who are successful and those who aren't is how one reacts to those valleys.

In sports, managers and coaches always talk about players committing to the process. A large part of this involves responding to and handling adversity. *How do we overcome a 21-3 half-time deficit? How do we overcome a 6-run first inning by the other team?* There is a process one must follow in order to overcome such obstacles. Just as clients have expectations for me as their agent, I have expectations for them. Unlike most agencies, I hold my clients accountable. If I'm going all-in, I have certain expectations involving their commitment to themselves, their community, their family, and my firm. Just like in the game, it's a team effort.

Ultimately, though I work with successful athletes, I want at-risk youth to know they needn't be a star athlete, musician, or actor to be a success story. Some people, like the client I mentioned, may escape a bad situation based on their inherent talent, but that is rare. Many more at-risk youths instead transcend their valleys by becoming valued citizens: teachers, doctors, lawyers, etc. I want those suffering in despair to know there is always a way out, even if it requires a lot of work. Knowledge gained from the challenge will bring them untold qualities imperative for long-term success.

Look. Life is hard. No doubt about it. However, tougher times can lead to better times if we continue to forge ahead—if we continue to learn from our setbacks. Those who are truly successful often *choose* to be successful while those who are not successful often *accept* failure as their reality. As I look back on my own early years, I see a highway littered with incredible obstacles: an impoverished childhood, physical abuse, mental abuse, emotional abuse, sexual abuse, multiple incarcerations in juvenile hall, and a complete lack of trustworthy allies. I could have easily quit, but I didn't.

Take my life as a lesson. If you believe in yourself and push forward, eventually something will happen in your favor. When that opportunity arrives, parlay that opportunity into success. Continue to climb the mountain. Do not focus on all of the negative noise. Instead, cling to the positive victories along the way. Make a conscious decision to change how you perceive what happens to you and remain steadfast in turning negatives into positives. Instead of believing your tank is two-thirds empty, be thankful you have one-third left, then use that one-third to fuel your endeavors. Finally, remember there will always be more excuses to fail than reasons to succeed. This is just the nature of life. How you respond to what happens to you—good or bad—will shape your results and who you become.

Epilogue

Seeing fireworks from inside an isolation cell made me realize I needed a change. I vowed to never miss another 4th of July fireworks show, and to this day, I haven't. Holidays have become such an important part of my life, especially when I get to share them with my lovely wife and my two sons.

When I saw Corbin for the first time, I knew I had many obligations as a father. When the nurse handed him to me in a wad of pastel linen blankets, I knew he was a bundle of potential—both for himself and for me. I wanted him to be successful, with a father to help lead the way. Even when I was rocking his mere eight pounds back and forth, I couldn't wait to play baseball with him, go fishing, and teach him how to ride a bike. I was going to make his birthday celebrations cool and teach him about life; I wanted his days to be filled with as many positive father-son moments as possible.

I felt the exact same way when Johnny was born. Throughout both of their childhoods, I made sure I was in the classroom, on the field, and at home to support them. I coached their baseball and flag football teams and volunteered in their elementary school classes. Perhaps one day they'll tell me they were mortified by my dad jokes or wisdom, but I knew I had to be there, and I hope they're glad I was too. As their coach, I tried to help them win every game, but if we lost, I used it as a learning experience.

My father's early death cracked my family's foundation. Lack of opportunity, combined with chronic abuse, led me to become a childhood criminal. When my sons were small, I had recurring nightmares of a premature death. It wasn't because I stressed over my own mortality. Instead, I worried how my early death would affect my children. On my own 12th birthday, Joe filled a gaping hole in my life by becoming a true father to me. I learned so many lessons from him; most importantly how to be an unselfish, caring, and loving dad. Fathers play so many roles in order to help their children be successful. I wanted to fulfill them all for my children. While I am grateful every day of the year to be a father, Father's Day is a particularly special reminder to me of how lucky I am to have the best job in the world.

Such lofty gratitude can be hard to summon when your child acts out or deliberately misbehaves. During these moments with my kids, I could easily revert back to the kinds of discipline I received. I could channel Tommy instead of who I truly am. Instead, I remember to be compassionate, yet firm. While I enjoy being close to my two boys, I don't consider myself to be just another one of their friends. I inhabit an important role requiring me to act with guidance, direction, and conviction—as well as a great deal of patience and understanding.

At the end of the day, I don't care if my children are the most popular kids in school. I don't care if my sons are the best players on the team or if they rank first in their graduating class. But I do care if they are respectful, kind, caring, and generous to others. I also expect them to commit 100% to everything they do; effort is more important than results during these formative years. *These* are the qualities I stress, not if they're 'winning.' I tell them: we speak for those who have no voice. We listen to those who have never been heard. We stand up for those who have been held down.

Similarly, I don't mind failure as long as they learn from it. I tell them not to repeat the action that led to failure. While it's hard to watch my children fail, it's more beneficial for them to learn how to get back up on their own.

When it comes to choices, I also ask my boys about their decisions rather than lecture them on what's right and wrong. In my opinion, their engagement in the right-versus-wrong decision arena forces them to contemplate different scenarios in which they can respond better—this is the foundation for real personal growth.

As for my own biological family's personal growth, each member has had their share of setbacks, their own trials and errors, as evidenced by this book. I have long since accepted the fact I am an outsider looking in on their lives.

My birth mother, Joan, passed away in January of 2016. Since I was fourteen, she lived in Section 8 housing. Our original home, tainted by misery and abuse, was eventually condemned by the city before my mother lost it to a tax lien. As a teenager, I often felt guilty for living in a beautiful home with Sandy and Joe while she lived in the projects. I always wanted to do more for her, but we were never able to reconcile in a way that I could. Tommy has been incarcerated most of his adult life. He is currently serving in the Florida State Penitentiary and should be released in 2020. Drugs and alcohol poisoned his life and killed any chance for accomplishments. He is now 52 years old and has one son, Tommy, Jr., who is a great example of persevering from a cycle of imprisonment. He didn't want to become like his father and worked hard to graduate college. I've always been very impressed by him.

Tommy's twin, Eddie, is a hard-working, blue-collar, hourly employee for housing and condo complexes. While he does not drink alcohol or use drugs, he endured a brutal marriage to an alcoholic and they separated ten years ago. She died recently from liver cirrhosis. They have two daughters from their marriage. Steve, my second oldest brother, is a firefighter and paramedic in South Florida. He has been married for thirty years, and, together, they have one daughter, Stephanie. Stephanie works as a social worker in South Florida. I like to think Stephanie is the social worker in the car who doesn't make too much small talk with the kids, yet demonstrates she's at least read their case file. She is just beginning her career and I have no doubt her compassion will yield exceptional results for the families she works with. Marie, my little sister, eventually received her GED after years of my urging and pushing. She works as an ambulance dispatcher in South Florida and has three kids with her husband, Tony.

When I was a junior in high school, Joe and Sandy had quite the surprise. Years earlier, Sandy and Joe gave up on ever having kids after many failed attempts, yet the pregnancy came unexpectedly. I was stoked when Joey was born as I finally had another chance to be a big brother. When he came to FSU, I would parade him around my fraternity house, trying my best to include him in my life. It's hard to catch him much nowadays, as he's busy with his own wife, newborn baby, and career. An exceptionally sharp accountant and CPA, Joey handles taxes for a number of my ballplayers.

After Joe suffered a massive stroke in late October 2011, I received a call from my mother. "Honey," she said, holding back tears, "Your father has had a major setback. The doctor said you should probably come home to see him."

I couldn't believe this was happening. My dad was just sixty-six years young and recently retired. He had a lot of living left to do. Here was a guy who dedicated his entire life to helping others—always placing everyone else's needs above his own—yet his life was about to be cut short. I boarded a flight, returning to South Florida.

I met my mother and brother, Joey, at the hospital. Other family members were present too. Entering the room, I saw my dad hooked up to life support. For one of the very few times in my life, I was shaken by something I couldn't control. I wanted to do something, but I knew my limitations. I knew I couldn't do anything to save my father's life. Though suffering, I had to maintain a strong presence for my mother and brother, so I choked back tears and began asking questions of the treating physicians. None of them had the answers I was hoping for. As my dad lay there motionless, I leaned over to whisper in his ear.

"Dad," I said, holding back my emotions. "It's me, Kurt. I know you can hear me so let me just say thank you for all you've done. I wouldn't be here without you." I briefly closed my eyes to collect myself. "Thank you for filling the role as my father—for teaching me how to be a father. Know my boys will benefit from your example. I love you, Dad."

At this moment, I realized I had a very difficult choice to make. While my mother understood the gravity of the situation, she was relying on me to make the final decision. It was the most difficult one of my life: deciding to end the life of the man who gave me a second chance. My mother, Joey, and I asked the other family and friends to leave the room so we could be alone with Dad one last time. We made the difficult decision together. The three of us spoke with Dad one last time, then told him it was okay to go. As we held onto each other, muttering these final words, my dad passed.

***

I honestly don't think I should be where I am today, but I am. I feel as if I'm living on borrowed time and, as such, I try to squeeze as many life experiences as possible into each day. For me, that involves finding time to help others, finding time to enjoy with my family, finding time to expand my education, and finding time to make myself better in every aspect of my life (physical, emotional and spiritual).

We often can't control what happens to us, but we can control our reactions. My experiences shaped my thought process, and I rely on hard-learned lessons to help the daily problems I face. Countless challenges have come my way, but I am still standing, and I have seen my hard work pay off. I'm a father, a husband, and a sports agent. Every day I'm doing what I want to do. I want to show others that despite abandonment, despite a troubling past, despite all of the hardships life throws at us, you too can do what makes you happy. You can react to life with unrelenting perseverance. You can learn from your mistakes and learn to trust yourself. Even if you are behind in the count, you can do more than just survive – you can thrive.

THE END

Photo Gallery

The oldest photo I have of my natural mother and father holding my twin older brothers, Tommy and Eddie.

The beginning of tough times to follow. Taken at my dad's funeral in April, 1973. From left to right are my mother, me (holding my mother's hand), my twin brothers Eddie and Tommy, and Steve.

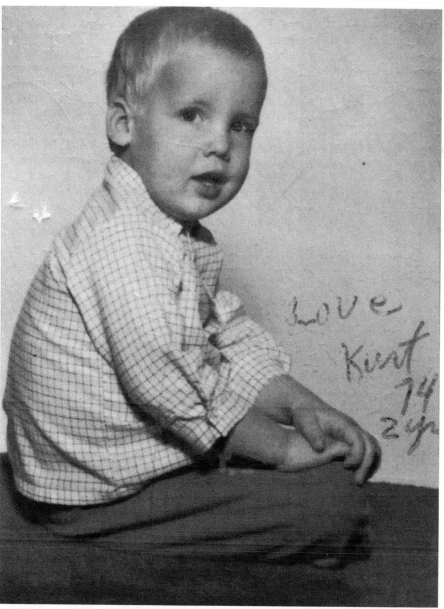

I don't have many photos from my youth, but this is me at 2 years-old.

My little sister, Marie, and me. Taken when I was 9 years-old, the photo shows our decaying home in the background.

Christmas Day, 1980. I had already been arrested several times and spent many nights on the streets. Within 2 months of this photo, I would be sentenced to my first stay in juvenile hall.

My little sister Marie and me during one of my respites from my juvenile escapades. I always tried to keep her close when I was home to protect her from harm.

I was placed with my foster parents, Joe and Sandy Evancho, on June 9, 1983. That summer, they took me on my first trip out of the state to New England. This photo is in front of Plymouth Rock.

Within a year of arriving at Sandy and Joe's, I was back in the game. Although I wasn't very good, I still played as hard as I could and had a better attitude than my previous baseball stint.

Attending my first Major League game in July 1986 at Fenway Park. Red Sox great, Jim Rice, gave me a baseball after he finished his pre-game warmups, cementing my love affair with this great game.

My first foray into the world of professional sports was under the guidance of Anita McDonald and the Kansas City Chiefs. Anita was one of the best marketing individuals in professional sports and instrumental in my early development.

Page 245

My foster parents, Joe and Sandy and my foster brother Joey at my law school graduation from the University of San Diego in June 2002.

Client Carlos Torres and I pose together. He was in AAA for the Las Vegas 51's (NY Mets affiliate at the time). A few weeks later, he was back in the Big Leagues.

Taking in the pre-game warmups from the dugout of the Nippon Ham Fighters at Marines Stadium in Chiba, Japan. In addition to handling MLB-related activities, I also send clients to play in Japan (NPB) and Korea (KBO) depending on where they are in their baseball careers.

As a father, I want to make sure I am always there for my family. This includes coaching my sons' Little League baseball teams. Here I am with both of my boys: Johnny (to the left) and Corbin (to the right).

My wife, Amy and me at the 2016 MLB All Star Game in San Diego, CA. She is, without a doubt, the family's rock and foundation.

In 2017, I had an opportunity to meet with Barbara Greenbaum, the social worker who placed me with Joe and Sandy Evancho. I cannot thank her enough for her tremendous help, especially in those early, challenging years.

JOHN A. MILLER
CIRCUIT JUDGE
SEVENTEENTH JUDICIAL CIRCUIT OF FLORIDA

BROWARD COUNTY COURTHOUSE
FORT LAUDERDALE, FLORIDA 33301

May 12, 1989

Mr. Kurt Varricchio

Plantation, Florida   33313

Dear Kurt:

Since signing your first Order of Community Control in 1980 and your subsequent "ventures" with Judge Polen, Judge Vitale, and Judge Moriarty, you certainly made a name for yourself in the juvenile division. Now you have made another name for yourself.

I was pleasantly surprised and very encouraged to read about you in last Monday's Fort Lauderdale News. Of course, I recognized your name immediately, so I did a little digging and found out the tremendous progress you have made since your first referral in 1979 to your current situation. I congratulate and commend you on this effort. I know it hasn't always been easy.

I cut the article out of the newspaper and have it on my wall in the Courtroom. I use it to show those who come in front of me that they don't have to have a dead end career. It is unfortunate that I cannot get all of the kids that I see to achieve the success that you have, but it does show that something can be done if the person makes an effort.

I understand that you have a hearing before Judge Birken on the 19th as a Dependency Review, and I know, of course, that there will be no problems there. Their are many that are pleased to see your achievements, not the least being Mr. and Mrs. Evancho. It is obvious that they have made a great effort on your behalf and that you have profited thereby. I know you appreciate what they have done.

Kurt, I just wanted to write and let you know that after hearing so much of the bad everyday, it's nice to hear some of the good. Congratulations and best wishes for your future success.

Sincerely,

JOHN A. MILLER

I received this letter from Circuit Court Judge John A. Miller just before my high school graduation. While I was honored to be recognized for making "another name" for myself, his use of my story to motivate other children is what sticks with me most.

Made in the USA
San Bernardino, CA
05 July 2018